*Nathan
Bush*

The
C.A.E.S.A.R.
Method

*Achieve Rapid
Strategic Growth With This 6 Step Process.*

Marketing Edition

The CAESAR Method (Marketing Edition):
Achieve Rapid Strategic Growth With This 6 Step Process.

Copyright ©2024 by Priority Investing, LLC. a Saint Louis Mo Company.

ISBN: 9798880069743

Contents

"If the last time you trained was in school, you are leaving thousands if not millions of dollars on the table."

- Nathan Bush

Introduction

"Without training, they lacked knowledge. Without knowledge, they lacked confidence. Without confidence, they lacked victory."

— *Julius Caesar*

As a child, I always felt like an outsider. Despite being at the top of my class academically, the social world of classrooms and playgrounds seemed alien to me. I loved sports but the players on the teams knew that I also loved to study. I did not fit in with them. In addition, the kids who studied knew about my passion for art and music. My passion for art and music seemed to keep me from making it into the smart kid groups because I was different. My true companions were books and theories, and within these pages, I found peace, connection, and inspiration. I immersed myself in various disciplines, sales, communication, marketing, leadership, language technologies, and history uncovering foundational principles that resonated within me. Yet, this sense of not fitting in became a silent badge I wore every day, a norm in my life.

This feeling of being an outsider stayed with me as I grew, but its nature evolved. I realized that my unique perspective was not a barrier but a bridge to understanding different groups and communities. I began to see patterns where others saw chaos and potential where others saw problems. It was in these moments that the concept of the CAESAR Method began to take root in my mind.

Entering the professional world, my approach was anything but conventional. I found that I wasn't the typical leader who commanded the spotlight. Instead, I thrived as the essential #2, the strategist and facilitator who turned visions into tangible successes. I saw myself as a Strategic Growth Facilitator, transcending the role of traditional coaching, consulting, mentoring, or training.

My focus shifted to integrating multiple disciplines to craft holistic growth strategies. This wasn't just about sharing knowledge; it was about creating a synergy between leadership, sales, marketing, customer service, and executive management to forge new paths for businesses.

The growth plans I developed were more than just documents; they were roadmaps for sustainable success. I helped organizations navigate the complex market landscapes, turning their uncertainties into opportunities. With the CAESAR Method, I provided an adaptable and forward-thinking framework, positioning both myself and the organizations I worked with as pioneers in their fields. Many of the companies grew fast and won multiple awards.

The most profound impact of my approach was seen in the communities I built within each organization. I fostered an environment of continuous learning and adaptation, empowering individuals and teams not just to improve but to evolve with the changing market dynamics.

This unique approach led these organizations to scale to well over six figures per month. My ability to facilitate growth and transform businesses from within became my signature in multiple industries: Healthcare, Real Estate, Insurance, and the Virtual Assistant Industry. In this process, I found my place. I realized that not fitting in wasn't about isolation but about preparing for a role that would redefine growth and success for many.

My journey from an outsider to a strategic builder of growth is a story of transformation. It shows that sometimes, not fitting in is exactly what is needed to create a space where everyone can fit in, grow, and thrive. In the end, my early days of feeling out of place were not a phase of isolation but a period of preparation for a role that would reshape the understanding of growth and success.

With the CAESAR Method, you are positioning yourself not just as a Leader, but as a Strategic Growth

Facilitator. This new market category transcends traditional coaching, consulting or training roles by combining elements of strategy development, mentorship, and innovative growth planning, specifically tailored for sales and marketing professionals.

Defining the New Category (The Strategic Growth Facilitator)

By positioning yourself as a Strategic Growth Facilitator, you're not just offering a service; you're creating a new paradigm in how executives, sales, and marketing professionals approach growth and strategy. This role puts you at the forefront of innovation in the field, much like how Steve Jobs redefined the music space with the iPod.

Integration of Multiple Disciplines: Unlike traditional coaching or training, your role as a strategic growth facilitator integrates your knowledge from various fields - leadership, sales, marketing, psychology, and language technology - to provide a holistic approach to growth.

Customized Growth Plans: Your focus will be on developing customized, actionable growth strategies for individuals and organizations, helping them navigate complex market landscapes more effectively.

Innovative Methodology: The CAESAR Method

provides a unique framework that is adaptable and forward-thinking, positioning you as a pioneer in your field, but your real secret weapon (Like a roman soldier is almost as old as time) is developing your team to implement the CAESAR method as part of your culture.

Facilitation of Sustainable Success: Your role is defined by its focus on long-term, sustainable growth for business, organization, employer, or clients, not just short-term gains.

Focus on Transformation and Adaptation: Emphasis on not just improving your existing skills, but also on cultivating everyone's commitment and understanding of the CAESAR method in the organization.

Positioning in the Market: You're not just reading another business strategy book; you're stepping into the role of a Strategic Growth Facilitator – a new position that sets a new gold standard in the realm of integrating the sales and marketing efforts.

This is more than a title; it's a distinct brand identity that elevates you above the traditional roles of coaching, consulting, and training. Think of it as redefining the game by not just playing it differently, but changing the rules in your favor.

Times have changed, but the principles for success have

not. Let me take you on a journey through the market landscape, just as I've experienced it. I'm here to share insights and educate you on the value and uniqueness of being a Strategic Growth Facilitator. Through thought leadership, engaging content, and the kind of success stories that make you lean in closer, I'll show you exactly why this role isn't just innovative – it's essential.

But what does all this mean for you and your business? I'll lay it out plain and simple by demonstrating the tangible value this approach has brought to the table. We'll explore case studies where strategy metamorphosed into success, where this framework became revenue, and where these ideas ignited industry innovation. And finally, this book is an invitation – no, let's call it a welcome call – to join an emerging community of sharp, forward-thinking strategic growth facilitators and the organizations who embrace the CAESAR method. Visit www.nathanbushmba.com/dol to join my community Disciples of Leadership.

It's about connecting with those who share your vision, your drive, and your determination to not just reach but exceed your loftiest business goals. You are going to transform your growth and thrive as a Strategic Growth Facilitator. So, are you ready to carve out your spot in the market as a Strategic Growth Facilitator? Let's turn this conversation into your reality. Let's start this journey together, right now, Let's Grow!

Note to the reader

(The CAESAR Method – Unlocking Your Potential in Strategic Growth Facilitation)

The CAESAR method is more than just a a framework; it's a map into the heart of effective growth. Whether you are a seasoned professional or just starting, the principles outlined here are designed to provide you with the tools and insights necessary to build your organization and scale with confidence.

Why the CAESAR Method?

In the fullness of time, under the dominion of Rome, three key elements facilitated the rapid expansion of an empire: political power that imposed order, military might that enforced control, and a vast network of roads that connected diverse peoples.

It was upon this very infrastructure, designed for conquest and control, that the Gospel of Jesus Christ traveled, a story not of subjugation but of liberation.

Rome, known for its pantheon of deities and emperors

who often claimed divine status, established a system where political leaders were not just heads of state but objects of worship. The power of Rome was absolute, its reach was long, and its roads were the veins through which the lifeblood of the empire flowed. These same roads, however, became conduits for a message that would challenge the very heart of Roman identity.

The teachings of Jesus Christ, rooted in Judaism yet revolutionary in their message of grace, forgiveness, and love, offered an alternative to the imperial cult.

Where Rome imposed order through might, the Gospel offered peace through sacrifice.

Where emperors demanded worship, Christ invited relationship.

And where the empire's roads facilitated legions and trade, they now enabled apostles and disciples to traverse the known world, sharing a Gospel that proclaimed freedom from oppression, grafting in non-jews to worship the one true God.

The early Christians, emboldened by the Great Commission, journeyed along the well-trodden Roman roads from Jerusalem to the far reaches of the empire. The Book of Acts in the New Testament chronicles these travels, especially those of the Apostle Paul, a Roman citizen who used his status to traverse borders and proclaim the risen Christ in synagogues, marketplaces, and before governors and kings.

God's sovereignty, it seemed, was using Rome's very ambition for His purposes. The Pax Romana, the Roman peace which made travel safer, and the common language of trade, Greek, used throughout the empire, facilitated the spread of a Gospel that transcended ethnicity, class, and creed. The message of Jesus Christ, which had humble beginnings in a manger in Bethlehem, now found its way into the heart of the empire, not by force, but by the power of its transformative message.

Thus, through the infrastructure of the mightiest empire of the time, the Gospel found a way, and the world was forever changed. From the roads that connected Rome, the message of a God who loved His creation enough to become part of it, who lived, died, and rose again, spread, offering not just a new religion, but a new way of life—the way of love, grace, and truth.

In a divine irony, the empire which sought to display its power through temples, arenas, and palaces became the stage for a far greater power—the power of the Gospel, which offered the world not another empire, but a kingdom; not another ruler, but a Savior.

And so, as the Roman Empire eventually faded into

history, the faith that once moved quietly along its roads grew into a global testimony, enduring and outlasting the very structures that had once seemed eternal. The Kingdom of God continued to advance, its King not seated on an earthly throne, but reigning in the hearts of believers across time and space.

"It always seems impossible until it's done," said Nelson Mandela. Mandela's journey from a prison cell to the presidency of South Africa serves as a testament to the power of enduring hope and the indomitable spirit of mankind to transcend limitations, reminding us that our greatest achievements often lie just beyond the bounds of our current belief. The CAESAR Method is an achievement and at the same time it's the culmination of years of experience, learning, and observation.

It is likely that you might recognize some of the principles in this book because the principles are timeless and don't change, but the difference is the framework is the fastest path to strategic growth and scanning any business or organization.

The CAESAR acronym is the backbone of my method, standing for Connection, Ask, Educate, Set the Intention, Align Interest, and Referrals. Think of it as the secret sauce to building a robust foundation, crafting impactful messages, and driving growth. This sequence isn't just a random assembly; it's a strategic formula applied across conversations, text messages, social media, video communications, webinars, and speaking engagements.

Following these steps, in this precise order, is like unlocking a door to commerce, fostering trust, and establishing lasting relationships with your audience. Each step is meticulously designed to guide you through engaging effectively, ensuring every interaction is a step towards success.

In the bustling heart of St. Louis, my first business endeavor. The first market I attempted to enter and my first journey in entrepreneurialism was as a young magician. I began, not only to perform but to connect, to understand, and to transform. This is my story, a testament to the power of the CAESAR Method, a framework that shaped my approach to magic and life.

I started each show not with a trick, but with a connection. I shared a bit of my story, my love for magic, and my excitement to be there. It was important for me to see the faces in the crowd, to feel their energy, and to let them feel mine. This wasn't just a performance; it was a shared experience, a moment of genuine connection.

"What type of magic do you want to see?" I would ask

my audience. This question opened a dialogue, revealing their desires and expectations. It wasn't just about what tricks they wanted to see; it was about understanding their perspectives, their dreams, and their idea of wonder, and opening the relationship with the audience.

With each card that disappeared and every object that appeared, I wasn't just performing tricks; I was educating. Not about magic secrets, but about the wonder of possibilities, the magic in believing that something extraordinary can happen. This was my way of showing that the real magic lies in our perceptions and beliefs.

My intention was always clear – to take my audience on an emotional journey. From the intrigue at the beginning, the suspense in the middle, to the awe and joy of the finale, every part of my act was designed to create a crescendo of emotions, much like how I guide my clients through transformative experiences in my Strategic Growth Facilitation.

My love for magic met their desire for wonder at a crossroads. I aligned my passion with their entertainment, creating a space where we could share in the experience. This alignment is akin to how I tailor my facilitation experience to resonate with the aspirations and intentions of my clients.

At the end of each performance, I encouraged my

audience, "If you enjoyed the magic, please tell others." This was an invitation to extend the joy and wonder they experienced, to share the magic beyond the walls of the venue. It reflects my belief in the organic growth of connections and the power of personal testimony, much like how I value referrals in my professional work.

This journey of mine, from a magician in St. Louis to a proponent of the CAESAR Method, is more than a story of tricks and illusions. It's a narrative about the art of engagement, the importance of emotional connections, and the transformative power of understanding your audience. It's a reflection of how the principles of the CAESAR Method are magical, creating explosive growth that appears to be an illusion but is very real. Keep in mind my goal was never to trick people but to cultivate a spirit of joy, excitement, and a little mystery in their lives.

And just like the magician, a Strategic Growth Facilitator has to keep companies focused on the growth, the result they would like, while making foundational changes to the way everyone speaks, thinks, and acts in the organization. The misdirection of a magician leads to a better relationship with the audience, the focus on growth provides you the opportunity to organize everyone in the business around the CAESAR Method.

Who Is This Book For?

This book is for anyone who aspires to grow a business, be a better leader, or a more impactful individual. Whether you are leading a team, marketing your business or someone else's, selling for an organization like a real estate brokerage, or all of the above, the CAESAR Method's framework guides you towards achieving your own personal growth intentions and theirs.

"This methodology has been highly effective at defining our services & how we can serve our potential clients. It puts our team in a position to have effective & successful presentation conversations with prospective clients." - David Howll, CEO of Red Maples, LLC. (Property Management)

"The CAESAR Method Marketing Edition has revolutionized the way we approach our leads. It's an essential tool for turning potential into profit. We have experienced explosive growth." - Michael Yablonowitz, CEO of BBC Global Services (Virtual Assistant)

What You Can Expect

We will explore each aspect of the CAESAR Method in detail. This process is used to explain the quickest way to influence someone to a mutually beneficial outcome. For the purpose of this book, we are going to show you the quickest way to build a relationship with someone, build trust, and put the relationship in position to create revenue from the interaction. No matter if you are in sales, marketing, leadership or customer service you can still use the CAESAR Method in any organization.

The CAESAR Method is:

- ☐ **Connection:** Most people can speak but few can create connection.
- ☐ **Ask:** Understanding precedes influence: listen first, lead second.
- ☐ **Educate:** Educate to empower: educate for forward movement.
- ☐ **Set the Intention:** Intention ignites progress: Boldly ask, thoughtfully advance.
- ☐ **Align Interest:** Harmony in purpose: Understand deeply, align closely.
- ☐ **Referrals:** Nurture your network: Every connection seeds future growth.

Your Path to Mastery

As you turn these pages, remember that the magic of mastery in any field is not what you tell people about what you can do, but who you are on the inside.

Your values determine your value. Remember that your inner mastery leads to your opportunity for market dominance. The spirit of growth transforms your interactions into opportunity. The CAESAR method is not "Rickem-Trickem-Rackem" techniques, manipulation, or dominance over people, like most sales and marketing approaches.

Use this book as a map or the instruction manual to the magic of growth, guiding you through the challenges and opportunities that lie ahead in your Strategic Growth Facilitation endeavors. You will be able to market and sales your services to align with the needs of others and you do not ever again have to feel like you are forcing, controlling, or injuring someone when they buy from you. You now have in your hands the exact way to grow with people, build revenue, open more relationships for your business.

For the purposes of character growth this method is not a trick, but a spirit that you will cultivate and helps grow any endeavor when you follow the CAESAR Method.

"Remember that your inner mastery leads to your opportunity for market dominance. The spirit of growth transforms your interactions into opportunity."

The CAESAR Method

The Five-Step Sales Strategy:

The 5 Keys to Dominating Your Market

My very first "real job" after college was selling hair care products for a national brand. From the moment I stepped into the world of hair care sales, I knew I was embarking on a journey unlike any other. It wasn't just about the products; it was about the stories, the dreams, and the transformations they enabled. My mission was clear from the start: to not just sell hair care products but to become a trusted advisor in the realm of beauty and self-care.

I remember the early days, filled with the hustle of calls, appointments, and presentations. Each interaction was a chance to learn more about my clients' needs and preferences. I wasn't just pushing a product; I was offering a solution, a way to enhance confidence and beauty. My approach was simple yet profound – listen more than you speak, understand deeper than the surface. This mantra saw me through countless interactions, slowly but steadily building a loyal client base.

My breakthrough came in a year of intense competition. Armed with a deep understanding of my products and a genuine desire to help, I crafted narratives that resonated with my clients. I recall one particular presentation where I shared a story about how our hair colour had transformed a client's self-esteem. The room was silent, the impact results. It was then that I realized the power of genuine, heartfelt communication.

Testimonials from satisfied clients started pouring in. Each review was a testament to the trust and relationships I had built. I meticulously gathered these endorsements, using them not just as sales tools but as educational stories of empowerment and transformation.

Just two years into my journey, I reached a milestone that still feels surreal. I was named the number one sales representative in the United States for the major national hair care brand I represented – not just once, but two years in a row. It was an accolade that went beyond numbers and targets; it was a recognition of the relationships I had nurtured and the value I had added to my clients' lives.

But my journey didn't stop there. I took this success as a cue to scale greater heights. I began mentoring new sales reps, sharing my insights and experiences. I wanted them to see beyond the traditional metrics of sales success and understand the deeper impact they could have on people's lives.

Today, as I look back, I realize that my success in hair

care sales was never just about the products. It was about understanding needs, building trust, and creating value that transcends the usual customer-seller relationship. It was a journey of growth, learning, and, most importantly, of making a real difference.

In the dynamic world of growth, the CAESAR method has emerged as a transformative approach to not just meet targets but to truly dominate the market. This five-step plan encapsulates the essence of this groundbreaking strategy. While it is important to note this 5 step formula is not the CAESAR method itself. It is critical in understanding how to scale your organization and use the CAESAR method to it's fullest.

Step 1: Build/Define Our Mission

The journey begins with clarity and conviction. Every sales team must understand the gravity of their roles—not just as revenue generators, but as ambassadors of the company's mission. It's imperative to articulate the narratives that define your corporate identity and the value of the services we provide. Crafting a written mission statement galvanizes the team, fostering a shared belief in the work you do, creating a foundation for success rooted in the company's positive impact.

To build this mission let me use a personal example from

our company at Red Maples. The team focuses on helping small multifamily real estate investors earn double digit returns with institutional-style property management.

Mission Statement:

"At Red Maples, our mission transcends the traditional boundaries of property management. We are deeply committed to empowering small multifamily real estate investors with the tools, insights, and strategies typically reserved for institutional players. Our focus is on driving double-digit returns for our clients through meticulous, strategic property management that maximizes property potential while maintaining the highest standards of tenant satisfaction and asset upkeep. We believe every investment property holds untapped potential, and our team is dedicated to unlocking this value, fostering long-term wealth and financial freedom for our clients."

Narrative for the Sales & Marketing Team: "In our role at Red Maples, we're not just managing properties; we're nurturing investments and dreams. We understand the aspirations of our clients and the trust they place in us with their multifamily investments. Our job is to make these investments work harder, smarter, and more efficiently, ensuring our clients not only see returns but also peace of mind. Every property we manage is an opportunity to demonstrate our commitment to our professionalism, proficiency and profitability. This contributes to the financial success of our clients."

"The only way to do great work is to love what you do." - Steve Jobs

Steve Jobs' quote resonates deeply with the narrative of Red Maples. In the context of the story, the team at Red Maples isn't just engaged in routine property management; they are passionate about transforming small multifamily real estate investments into lucrative ventures. This passion for their work is what drives them to go beyond the norm and deliver exceptional results.

Steve Jobs, a visionary in his field, understood that passion is a critical component of success. The relevance of his words to the Red Maples scenario lies in the fact that it's their love for what they do that enables them to provide such high-quality, detailed, and strategic management services. Their passion for real estate and investor success is what sets them apart and drives them to achieve outstanding results for their clients.

Do you have a mission statement?

When I was a Strategic Growth Facilitator for the hair care company I would often be heard saying, "I can't walk on water, I can't help the blind see, nor can I heal the cripple, but I can help people feel at their best!" A mission is a belief requirement in your product or service. For the CAESAR Method to be effective you MUST know who you serve and what problem your product or service heals.

Step 2: Build in C.A.P.S.A.R Tracking

Calls. Appointments. Presentations. Sales. Average Sales Price. Referrals—our mantra for progress. This tracking demands the team's full commitment. It's not enough to perform tasks; we must embody the principles that drive our client interactions. Daily reports are not mere paperwork; they are diagnostic tools that reveal where we thrive and where we require support.

As a young sales professional, I remember the day I truly understood the essence of sales. It wasn't during a big presentation. It was a regular Tuesday afternoon, and I was looking over my weekly numbers: calls, appointments, presentations, and the rest. That's when it hit me - these numbers weren't just about tracking; they were about understanding and growth.

Remember Steve Jobs said, "The only way to do great work is to love what you do." This quote resonated with me that afternoon. I realized that my passion wasn't just about closing deals; it was about the journey - the calls I made, the appointments I set, the presentations I delivered, and the relationships I built.

Have you ever stopped to think about how your daily activities in sales reflect your passion and commitment?

Sales is not just a series of tasks and magic words to be checked off. It's an art that requires understanding, adapting, and refining. C.A.P.S.A.R - Calls, Appointments, Presentations, Sales, Average Sales Price, Referrals - is a testament to this art. Each element is a step in the journey towards sales mastery.

Do you track these numbers? If you don't I can tell you why you are not growing. If you do then I can tell you where your system is not working.

Tracking calls is more than just the numbers you dial, this tells me exactly how many leads you have and about how many connections you are making. Appointments are opportunities to understand client needs. Presentations are platforms to showcase value. Sales are the culmination of efforts, but they're also the start of new relationships. The Average Sales Price reflects the value perceived by your clients, and Referrals are the ultimate indicator of their trust in you

But how do you ensure you're making the most of these elements? The key is tracking and reflection. By keeping a close eye on these metrics, you understand not just your performance but also your growth areas. It's about aligning these metrics with your core values and the needs of your clients.

This is where the CAESAR method becomes invaluable. It's not just a tracker; it's a guide. It helps you navigate through your growth process with a clear purpose. When you align your efforts with this method, you're not just working; you're crafting a path to excellence.

So, do you know someone who could benefit from understanding and implementing this tracking in their C.A.P.S.A.R? Perhaps a colleague or a friend in the sales field? Referrals are a powerful tool, not just in business but in sharing knowledge and success strategies.

The CAESAR method is more than a sales strategy; it's a journey towards personal and professional excellence. It's about embodying the principles that drive successful client interactions and using our daily activities as tools for growth and reflection. Let's embrace this journey with passion and purpose, just as Steve Jobs did, and transform our sales approach into an art form.

Step 3: Build the Scripts, Assessments, Presentations, and Offer.

I still remember my early days in sales, sitting across from potential clients, feeling a mix of excitement and nervousness. One particular day stands out. I had prepared meticulously, yet the conversation veered off in an unexpected direction. That day I learned a vital lesson: successful sales are a process and are about much more than just talking; they're about connecting, understanding, and responding effectively.

Henry Ford once said, "If there is any one secret of success, it lies in the ability to get the other person's point of view and see things from that person's angle as well as from your own." This insight is at the heart of the CAESAR method, a transformative approach to client conversations.

Have you ever considered how your approach to client dialogue might be impacting your sales results?

The CAESAR Method teaches the importance of crafting conversations that are not only influential but also empathetic. It's a tool to value people. It's not a win-lose or lose - lose, or even lose - win approach. It's an alignment of interests to heal the pain another is experiencing.

The Call to Appointment Script, for instance, is your first opportunity to engage a potential client. It's not just about getting them to agree to a meeting; it's about starting a relationship. How you handle this initial interaction sets the tone for everything that follows.

If you're struggling to convert **appointments into proposal presentations**, it's time to reassess your approach. Are you truly addressing the client's needs and concerns? Are your presentations tailored to show how your intentions align to heal their pain?

When it comes to getting revenue with setting your intentions, **your offer strategy** is crucial. This isn't just about the price or the features of your product or service; it's about the value it brings to the client. Are you effectively communicating this value?

Finally, driving your **Average Sales Price and Referrals** hinges on your long-term assessment process. Are you continually assessing and responding to your clients' evolving needs? Are you building relationships that foster trust and lead to referrals?

The CAESAR method isn't just a set of techniques; it's a mindset shift. It's about understanding that every aspect of client interaction, from the initial call to long-term follow-up, contributes to your overall success.

As you implement this method, keep track of each element - calls, appointments, presentations, sales, and referrals. Observe how changes in your approach impact your results.

Do you know someone struggling to make their mark in sales? Share the CAESAR method with them. It's a game-changer for anyone looking to improve their client interactions and sales results.

In the end, influence is an art form where empathy, understanding, and adaptability reign supreme. The CAESAR method is your guide to mastering this art, transforming every client conversation into an opportunity for successful alignment with your ability to heal their pain.

Engaging with clients is like painting a masterpiece; every stroke, every color choice matters. It's about crafting dialogues that not only speak but resonate, and conducting assessments that go beyond the surface to uncover real needs. This is where the magic of the CAESAR Method comes into play – it's your palette and brush in the art of influential conversation.

Imagine the **Call to Appointment Script** as the first bold stroke on your canvas. This isn't just any script; it's the golden key to unlocking more appointments, the very lifeblood of your sales. It's where you start to address the puzzle of why appointments might not be turning into sales.

Now, let's say you're getting those appointments, but the sales just aren't following. Here, the CAESAR Method shines a light on your **proposal presentations**. It's like stepping back and looking at your painting – what needs to change? Is your offer as compelling as it could be?

But what about when you're collecting revenue, yet your

Average Sales Price or Referrals aren't where they should be? It's time to zoom out for a wider view, examining your long-term assessment process. This is about fine-tuning, adding those details that turn a good painting into a great one.

The CAESAR Method isn't just an influence technique; it's a transformative approach that turns every interaction into a potential relational outcome masterpiece. With this method, every call, every appointment, and every presentation is an opportunity to create something memorable and impactful.

Step 3: Build the Scripts, Assessments & Presentations

Calls	Appointments	**The Phone Conversation**	Sales	Average Sales Price	**The Offer Strategy**
Appointments	Presentations	**The Assessment: Meeting 1**	Average Sales Price	Referrals	**The long term assessment process**
Presentations	Sales	**The Presentation: Meeting 2**			

The 5 Step Plan: The Keys to Dominating Your Market

31

Step 4: Build a Bank of Testimonials

Nothing speaks louder than the voices of your satisfied clients. In the realm of faith, testimonies are powerful tools of connection and transformation. They are stories of personal journeys, pain healed, and profound moments of revelation that inspire and uplift the community. Drawing from this rich tradition, we view our bank of testimonials not merely as endorsements but as modern-day testaments of healing. Each video, narrative, case study, and review is akin to a testimony shared from the pulpit – a deeply personal account of struggle, discovery, and ultimately, triumph.

These testimonials resonate with those who are seeking answers, guidance, or relief from their own professional or business-related pain points. Just as religious testimonies can move congregants to a deeper understanding or conviction, our clients' stories illuminate the path for others. They showcase not just the efficacy of our methods but the emotional and strategic journey we embark on with each client, highlighting our role in guiding them through their challenges towards a place of success and fulfillment.

By sharing these testimonials, we open a dialogue about healing – not just in the spiritual sense, but in the practical, actionable realm of business growth and leadership. They serve as beacons of hope for those grappling with similar issues, demonstrating that with the right guidance, their pain can be understood and addressed. In this way, our testimonials become more than just marketing tools; they are our modern-day parables, stories that help others see how we can help them heal, grow, and thrive.

Step 5: Scaling the System

And here we are, at the heart of your growth strategy, where every step we take is intentional. We've built a recruitment and training system that doesn't just bring in top talent; it cultivates a team destined for more than just sales success.

They're recruited to shatter financial goals and redefine what success means. Our approach?

A scalable system that leverages webinar training, equipping your staff with the skills they need to excel not only on the sales floor but in every aspect of their professional lives.

It's about empowering each team member to reach heights they hadn't imagined possible, transforming their job into a journey of holistic career development. You have to train your staff on the CAESAR Method.

The Mentality

"Transform setbacks into success using the
setback as the reason to succeed." - Nathan Bush

In this chapter, we're going to talk about the most
important piece of your growth. Nothing is as crucial as
this aspect of your revenue generation process and
ability to scale to success: the power of resilience.

As we journey through your mentality, remember the
words of basketball legend Michael Jordan: "I've failed
over and over again in my life. That's why I succeed."
This powerful sentiment lays the foundation for our
discussion today.

Before you read on too much more, ask yourself the
question, "Why is this quote so critical to this lesson?"

Embracing the Challenge: In the world of revenue
generation and acquiring new clients, appointment
setting is critical. Appointment setting turns your leads
into opportunities. You will gain rejections and setbacks
as par for the course. Each 'no' we encounter isn't a
roadblock but a stepping stone, an opportunity for
learning and growth. It's critical to see every rejection
as a chance to refine our approach, hone our skills, and

ultimately, pave our way to success. The designing communication scripting for setting appointments is kinda like building roads. Each section of the CAESAR method opens up all the benefits of growth in your organization. Setting appointments are key to growth and require resilience against a lot of potential "rejection." I put this in quotes because when executed correctly, there is not rejection but really you gain understanding that there is no alignment with your offer.

Since we are going to need a resilient mindset, there are only two ways to build a resilient mentality; an offensive strategy and defensive strategy for resilience.

Your Offensive Strategy Checklist:

☐ **Embrace Challenges:** Welcome every challenge as an opportunity. When faced with a setback, know that each person you sort as not interested right now brings you closer to someone who is looking for your help.

☐ **Celebrate Small Victories:** It's the little wins that keep us going. Each positive step, no matter how small, deserves recognition and celebration.

☐ **Maintain a Positive Attitude:** A positive mindset can be your strongest ally. Approach each appointment with optimism and see how it transforms your results.

☐ **Learn from Failures:** Failure is not the opposite of success; it's part of it. Reflect on your failures, learn from them, and move forward with new insights.

☐ **Focus on Your Intentions:** Keep your eyes on the prize. Your intentions are your motivation; let them drive you forward.

No coach in National Football League history achieved more success in less time than Lombardi did during his nine seasons as the head coach of the Green Bay Packers. As Vince Lombardi once said, "The difference between a successful person and others is not a lack of strength, not a lack of knowledge, but rather a lack of will." This quote perfectly encapsulates the essence of the offensive mindset it takes to succeed. Legendary football coach Bear Bryant is credited with saying: "Offense wins games … defense wins championships." Now you need the defensive strategies to win.

Your Defensive Strategies Checklist:

☐ **Positive Self-Talk:** Begin your day affirming your abilities. Remind yourself of your skills and your capacity to achieve your intention.

☐ **Reframe Negative Thoughts:** Convert setbacks into opportunities for growth. Shift your focus from what went wrong to what can be learned.

☐ **Build Resilience:** Resilience is the hallmark of success. Learn to quickly recover from setbacks, keeping a positive and forward-looking attitude.

☐ **Believe in Your Service:** Passion for your product or service is contagious. Believe in its value and convey that belief to your clients.

"The CAESAR Method transforms talent into top performers, crafting careers that transcend expectations."

Practical Exercise:

Reflect on a recent setback. What was your initial reaction?

How did it affect your mindset?

Now, reframe this experience into a positive learning opportunity.

Write down these insights and use them in your next calls. Share your experiences in our Disciples of Leadership group, detailing both the challenge and how you turned it into a positive outcome @ www.nathanbushmba.com/dol

Remember, developing a winning mindset is a journey, not a destination. With consistent effort, a positive attitude, and an openness to learning, you'll not only meet your goals but exceed them. Resilience is more than just a trait; it's a skill that we can all develop and strengthen. By embracing challenges, celebrating victories, maintaining positivity, learning from our failures, and staying goal-oriented, we equip ourselves for success in appointment setting and beyond.

Let's step out there with confidence and resilience. Here's to making today a great day in our sales journey!

Influence is about controlling yourself and adding value to others. Most people have this backwards!

Kickoff Training Session
To Launch the CAESAR Method:
Effective Prospect Engagement with the CAESAR Method

Objective: To enhance lead and sales conversions, increase Average Sales Price (ASP), and foster repeat business using the CAESAR Method.

Step 1: *Compile a Prospects List:* Begin by creating a comprehensive list of your prospects. Ensure this list is up-to-date with the latest contact information.

Step 2: *Segregate Prospects Based on Account Status:* Separate your prospects into two categories: those who owe a balance and those who do not. Those who can buy from you and those who can't. This will help in tailoring your approach for each group effectively.

Step 3: *Legal and Ethical Outreach:* Initiate contact through legal methods: phone calls, text messages, and emails. Remember to adhere to all legal guidelines pertaining to customer outreach.

Step 4: *Persistent Yet Respectful Follow-up:* If there's no response, follow up with a second phone call. Persistence is key, but it's important to be respectful of the prospect.

Step 5: *Tactful Pursuance:* During your conversations, tactfully navigate the discussion towards agreement on the next step with your company. Your approach should be understanding yet assertive, ensuring the prospect acknowledges you asked for the next step while maintaining a positive relationship.

Step 6: *Secure an Appointment:* Do you best to use what you know to ask them to set an appointment. Regardless of where they are in the sales process the goal is to work on setting an appointment.

Conclusion and Reminder: Implementing these steps with diligence and tact will significantly enhance your engagement with prospects. The CAESAR Method is not just a tool for securing appointments; it's a comprehensive approach to building lasting customer relationships and driving growth. Remember, the goal is not only to resolve outstanding issues with these prospects or clients but also to create a pathway for future business opportunities.

This session underscores the importance of systematic prospect engagement, combining legal and ethical outreach with persistent and tactful communication strategies. With the CAESAR Method, you're well on your way to achieving higher conversion rates, increased sales, and long-term client relationships. Let's put this into practice and watch our success grow!

The Unconquerable Mindset of Rome's Finest (Invictus Mentis)

"The Law of The Mirror: You Must See Value In Yourself And Add Value To Yourself"
- John Maxwell, 15 Invaluable Laws of Growth

Within the walls of ancient Rome, the mightiest warriors weren't just strong in body but also indomitable in spirit. They knew the battlefield was as much mental as it was physical. This philosophy is the bedrock of the CAESAR method—an appointment setting approach I crafted to increase the odds of success in the modern-day colosseum of growth.

As I recall, the genesis of the CAESAR method was not just an epiphany but a culmination of experiences, a reflection of the Law of The Mirror that John Maxwell speaks of. I learned early on that valuing oneself is the first step toward adding value to yourself.

In my career I learned you have to invest in yourself first. People who invest in themselves see value in themselves and this investment is adding value to themselves. I have worked to do this process all my life. You cannot grow a business or organization until you first grow yourself. *Your business will never outgrow your self worth.*

Ways I have made investments in myself have been as follows:
Audio Books: Over $5,000 (ish)
Books: Over $10,000 (ish)
Seminars: Over $20,000 (ish)
Workshops: Over $30,000 (ish)
Mentors and Programs: Over $40,000 (ish)
College Undergrad and MBA Over $50,000 (ish)
Life experience in sales and marketing Priceless.

I have used round numbers and the suffix "ish" because I do not have the exact numbers for these things but I can tell you I have invested well over $155,000 in my personal development. I have not done the math in what this quotes to in todays dollars either. Just know it's a lot of investment. And so, I endeavored to create a process based on all this study that mirrored the strength and strategy of Rome's finest.

Connecting with the Past, Leading to the Future:
"All you need is the plan, the roadmap, and the courage to press on to your destination," said Earl Nightingale, a man whose voice resonated through the radios and hearts of many, including mine as I listened to his audio

programs. His wisdom was a beacon that led me to realize the power of a well-laid plan—a roadmap akin to the CAESAR method that would guide salespeople through the twists and turns of client interactions.

Mapping the Journey: The CAESAR Method

C - Connect: My early days as a salesperson taught me the essence of connection. I remember reaching out, not with just a script, but with a genuine interest in who I was speaking to, finding common ground even before discussing business.

A - Ask: I learned to ask one power question that brought up the outcome I was looking to see, this way I did not mislead or deceive anyone. Questions set us closer to uncovering their true needs of our potential clients.

E - Educate: With each interaction, I found joy in sharing client success stories and industry facts, in educating my prospects about how our products or services heald their pain. It was about offering healing.

S - Set the Intention (Appointment): The pivotal moment was always setting the intention, akin to a general planning the next move in a campaign. It was about timing, precision, and anticipation of what was to come. Disclosed intentions open relationships.

A - Align Interests: Alignment of interests was where

deals were won or lost. I remember countless discussions, ensuring that what we offered was in perfect sync with the client's intentions.

R - Referrals: And finally, it was about building an army of advocates, those who would speak of our partnership and recommend our services to others, much like the messengers of old, spreading tales of Roman triumphs.

The Essence of Personal Interaction: The importance of personal interaction was a lesson taught by history. Rome wasn't built in isolation; it was built on relationships, alliances, and a shared vision. As Strategic Growth Facilitators , we embody the frontline soldiers, understanding that the art of our role extends far beyond a simple pitch—it's about strategy, communication, and most importantly, building lasting relationships.

The Marathon of Growth: I often tell my team that intention setting is a marathon, not a sprint. It requires the same endurance and strategy as Rome's finest preparing for a long campaign. Each appointment is a mile conquered, each relationship a victory claimed. Negotiation is not winning the argument, but in winning the relationship.

Reflection: *To see value in yourself you are going to have to reflect on your journey.*

The Heart of Influence: In the quiet moments, I reflect, much like the philosophers of ancient Rome, understanding that a lack of reflection can cloud your vision, and can cause you to miss the lessons hidden within each challenge and triumph.

Exercises for the Legion: I encourage my team to share why their roles on the team are so crucial to growth, and we discuss the nuances that distinguish them from the rest of the company. We review the importance of their process they follow. It's about understanding the 'why' as much as the 'how.'

Scoring the Self: And so, as leaders, as warriors in the field of Growth, we must constantly assess ourselves.

- How well do we connect with our team & potential team members?
- Are we asking the right questions of our team and those we are looking to hire?
- How effective are our education efforts to train and develop our team?
- Are we intentions that lead to success, and are we leveraging the power of team intention setting
- How effective are we aligning the interests of the staff with the goals of the organization?
- How good are we at getting referrals from the team for clients and potential team members?

The CAESAR Method is more than a strategy; it's a philosophy that champions the unconquerable mindset — Invictus Mentis. It's about seeing value in ourselves, adding value to ourselves so we can better serve clients, and ultimately, lead our businesses to triumphant growth.

"Forge alliances, conquer fears, and celebrate victories – all in a day's work with the CAESAR Method!"

The Law of The Mirror
Self-Value and Service Value

Objective: Understand the importance of self-perception in providing value to clients.

Key Activities: Self-assessment exercises to gauge self-perception. Interactive discussion on John Maxwell's "15 Invaluable Laws of Growth." You'll be developing a personal growth plan. In this training exercise, we'll embark on a journey of self-discovery to understand how our self-perception directly influences our ability to provide value to clients.

The Law of The Mirror, as elucidated by John Maxwell, teaches us that our self-worth is the mirror through which our professional value is reflected. You have to see value in yourself to add value to yourself. We'll engage in introspective self-assessment exercises aimed at uncovering our core beliefs about ourselves.

Through these activities, we will identify areas where our self-view needs polishing and develop strategies to enhance our self-image, ensuring that the value we perceive within ourselves is the value we project in servicing our clients. Reflecting on "The Law of the Mirror," which teaches that you must see value in yourself to add value to yourself, consider these questions to deepen your understanding and application of the principle:

Self-Reflection: What are three qualities or skills that I possess which I believe add significant value to my interactions with clients?

Growth Assessment: In what areas do I feel I need to grow to enhance the value I offer to those I serve?

Impact Evaluation: How does my current self-perception affect my professional performance and the way I engage with clients?

Value Recognition: Can I identify a recent situation where recognizing my own value led to a positive outcome in my work?

Feedback Analysis: What is the most constructive feedback I have received, and how have I used it to see more value in myself?

Client Perception: How do I think my clients currently perceive the value I bring to them, and what can I do to improve or change that perception?

Growth Plan: What specific steps will I take to work on the areas of personal growth I have identified?

Value Addition: How can I use my strengths more effectively to add value to every client interaction?

Overcoming Insecurities: What insecurities do I have that might be preventing me from fully valuing myself, and how can I address them?

Legacy Consideration: How do I want to be remembered by my clients and colleagues, and how does this relate to the value I see in myself and the value I give?

Connect

(Connections are the currency of growth — invest wisely and watch your influence expand.)

There's a tradition in our home that's a surefire ticket to a night of peaceful slumber - back scratches. Not your ordinary, half-hearted scratch. No, no. We're talking about a meticulously executed symphony of soothing scratches that lulls you into a state of blissful tranquility.

One night, we were all nestled in, prepping for the sacred ritual of sleep. My daughter, her eyes wide with anticipation, was eagerly awaiting her customary back scratch. She had come to relish this nightly routine, not unlike a queen awaiting her royal entourage.

But, you see, there comes a time in every parent's life when they're running on their last ounces of energy, their limbs asking, begging, for respite. Such was the case that night. So, in a moment of what can only be described as parental ingenuity, her mother turned to her and said, "Why don't you go scratch your back on the door frame?"

My daughter's eyes widened in what I'm pretty sure was a mix of disbelief and horror. Her response was priceless. With all the indignation an affronted mini-queen could muster, she exclaimed, "I'm not a Barbarian or a Bear!"

I couldn't help but laugh. Of course, the idea of her imitating a bear in the woods, rubbing her back against a tree (or in this case, a door frame), was amusing. But what really got me was the sheer affront she felt at the suggestion. Her prim little declaration that she was, indeed, not a barbarian or animal, will remain one of those endearing, hilarious moments that I will cherish, and retell, forever.

"People don't care how much you know until they know how much you care." - John C. Maxwell

John C. Maxwell's words resonate with me as I reflect on my journey to learn connection. His emphasis on the relational aspect of connection echoes the core of the CAESAR Method —a strategy to forge not just connections but meaningful relationships with prospects. By the end of this chapter my hope is that you have peace and are not afraid to make a new connection with someone.

Have you determined the who, what, when, where, why, and how to connect with others?

This question lays the groundwork for establishing

rapport, a term that goes beyond mere interaction to signify a deeper, more harmonious relationship. According to Webster, to connect is "to have or establish rapport," which is further defined as a relationship characterized by agreement, mutual understanding, or empathy, thereby making communication possible or easy.

But what underpins this sense of rapport that is so crucial for connection? It turns out that the answer might lie within the very fabric of our biology. Research highlighted by Paul J. Zak in 2017 reveals a fascinating aspect of human nature: our brains secrete a chemical known as oxytocin, which, as Zak points out, "appeared to do just one thing—reduce the fear of trusting a stranger (Zak, 2017)." This discovery illuminates the biological basis of how we establish connections, suggesting that oxytocin plays a pivotal role in building rapport. Essentially, this chemical acts as a bridge, fostering trust between individuals, which is the foundation upon which rapport is built.

Understanding this connection between oxytocin and trust offers a profound insight into the mechanics of human relationships. Rapport, then, is not merely a social construct but is deeply rooted in our neurological makeup. The presence of oxytocin reduces barriers to trust, making it easier for individuals to connect on a meaningful level. This realization brings to light the importance of trust in the process of connecting with others. Without trust, establishing a mutual understanding or empathy, key components of rapport, becomes significantly more challenging.

Therefore, as we navigate the complexities of connecting with others, it's vital to consider the role of trust and the biological mechanisms that support it. By fostering environments that encourage the release of oxytocin, such as through positive social interactions and the creation of safe, welcoming spaces, we can enhance our ability to connect with others. This understanding not only enriches our personal relationships but also has profound implications for professional environments, where trust and rapport are essential for collaboration and success.

The journey to connect with others is intricately linked to our ability to establish trust. By embracing the insights provided by science, particularly the role of oxytocin, we can better understand the foundational elements of rapport. This knowledge equips us with the tools to create deeper, more meaningful connections, enriching both our personal and professional lives.

The Roman Way - A Modern Take
The Romans were masters of social engagement, gathering in their marketplace and theater, not merely to conduct business but to build strategic relationships

that lasteted. They celebrated together, debated, and built alliances through shared experiences. I realized that these ancient practices had a place in modern growth strategies.

Emulating Rome's Most Influential Rebel

In my own experience, I've found that our strategies in connecting with clients need not be different from how One of the greatest influencers of all time built their following:

- [ ] **Public Speaking and Storytelling:** Like this influential orator, captivating an audience, weaving narratives that strike chords with potential clients, making the connection personal and the conversation memorable.

- [ ] **Acts of Service:** Going beyond the call of duty and showing genuine care for others' well-being helps cement lasting bonds.

- [ ] **Cross-Cultural Interactions:** Embracing diversity and showing genuine interest in others' backgrounds is invaluable for building rapport in today's global marketplace.

- [ ] **Personal Connection with Alliance & Authenticity:** This teacher deepened connections through shared meals and experiences, surrounding himself with 12 followers from varied backgrounds, akin to today's brand ambassadors. Their diversity amplified his teachings' reach.

Overcoming Barriers to Connection

In the connection process, I've encountered barriers to connection: lack of maturity, excessive self-importance, neglecting to value everyone, and self-doubt. To overcome these, I focused on:

Connecting with others,
Maintaining a positive attitude,
Communicating selflessly

Every prospect asks, "Do you care about me? Can you help me? Should I trust you?" It's our job to answer these questions affirmatively, not with words but with our actions.

After the Interaction: Reflection and progress
In my earliest days of cold calling, I'd often ask myself why people weren't listening or aligning with me. It took time to realize that the problem lay not with them but with me. I learned that to truly connect, I had to focus less on myself and more on them. It's not about me.

Connecting was not about me, and if you are going to connect you have to realize it's not about you. When you are making your first call or interaction you must connect and everyone has the same script so you have to be memorable.

Here is the basic connect script you can follow. We will build on to this script but you have to learn the basics of introducing yourself. Tell your connections who you are, the company you work for, your position or role, the pain you can heal, and the key result you can deliver, and why you are connecting with them specifically.

"Hello, my name is [Your Name], and I'm with [Company Name]. I am a Growth Facilitator and We specialize in [The pain you can heal] that helps businesses like yours achieve [Key Result]. (Referral) told me that we should connect.

This introduction is't just a script, it is the beginning of a relationship. It must be true and not deceitful. Lead your connection with honesty. You are going to build onto this script with the following sections.

Deepening the Connection
There are some language technologies I've employed to release Oxcitocin and deepen connections and improve the connection script:

1. Using powerful words to capture attention,
2. Finding common interests.
3. Leveraging group affiliations,

Alert How to Use powerful words to capture attention: To connect, news flash, you also need to gain people's attention! Why should they have a conversation to being with? When connecting, the exciting words you use can play a big role in capturing the attention of potential clients. One word that is often effective in getting someone's attention is "alert." When you use the word "alert," you immediately grab the listener's attention and create a sense of urgency.

Some other words and phrases that can be effective in getting someone's attention in appointment setting include:

- Urgent
- Breaking News
- Exclusive
- Limited Time Offer
- New
- Attention
- Required
- Important
- Don't Miss Out
- Now
- Immediate
- Quick
- Responsibility

- You
- Free
- Immagine
- Last Chance
- Proven
- Safe
- Guarentee
- Transform
- Community
- Join
- Family
- Support
- Together

As you can see you will need to refine your connect script depending on the situation and what are your intentions. How many of these words do you use when you meet someone for the first time? Using connecting words are one way to connect but combine this with finding common interests.

Finding common interests: To establish a genuine connection with a prospect on a personal level can help to build connection and establish trust. While it's essential to respect professional boundaries and maintain relevance to the conversation's purpose, the following are 12 topics that can serve as icebreakers or conversation starters:

☐ **Local News or Events:** Discussing local happenings can be a great way to establish common ground, especially if you and the prospect live in the same area or if the prospect's business is affected by these events.

☐ **Industry News:** While this can be somewhat business-related, it's more about the broader industry trends and news which may affect both your business and theirs. It shows you're knowledgeable and up-to-date.

☐ **Sports:** Sports is a common topic that many people can relate to. If you're aware that your prospect is a fan of a particular team or sport, this can be an excellent topic to discuss.

☐ **Weather:** It's clichéd but the weather can be a neutral, non-controversial topic to break the ice. It works best when there's something notable happening (a heatwave, a snowstorm, etc).

☐ **Holidays or Seasonal Events:** This can include anything from asking about their plans for the upcoming holiday, their thoughts on the Super Bowl halftime show, or what they think of the latest popular summer blockbuster.

☐ **Travel:** If you know that they have recently been on a trip, asking about their experience can allow them to share personal stories.

☐ **Books, Movies, and TV Shows:** These are universal topics that most people can relate to. If you know they have a particular interest, this can make for good conversation.

☐ **Hobbies and Interests:** If you've learned from previous conversations or their social media profiles that they have a specific hobby or interest, this can be a great topic.

☐ **Food and Drink:** If you know they enjoy a particular cuisine or drink, this can be a fun and light-hearted topic.

☐ **Charities or Causes:** If you know that the prospect is passionate about a particular charity or cause, showing genuine interest in their involvement can help to create a connection.

☐ **A cleaver introduction:** If you can make the prospect smile you are 1/2 way there to connecting.

☐ **A specific personal follow up:** You can connect when you truly have a reason to call someone.

My intention with initial conection conversations is to use these topics prior to my script. It is very brief when possible but I certainly use them in my script if I cannot use them right up front.

Leveraging group affiliations: One way to warm up a connection is to leverage affinity groups. People want to see that you are invested in them. They want to see you have things in common. We can show this by connecting around affiliations. You must go to them. You cannot wait for them to try and connect with you. You must genuinely be connecting around some of these things.

Affinity groups are social groups formed around a common interest or shared characteristic. They are formed when individuals have a common goal, interest, or background and come together to achieve that goal.

In the context of sales and marketing, affinity groups can refer to groups of people who share similar interests or demographics and can be targeted as a market segment. By understanding and targeting these groups, companies can better understand their customers and create more effective marketing campaigns that resonate with them.

By creating a sense of belonging and community, affinity groups can be a powerful tool for building brand loyalty and driving sales. An Affinity Group is a group of individuals who share similar interests, values, or experiences. This can be leveraged by appointment setters to create a connection with potential clients and increase the chances of setting an appointment. Here are a few examples of how to connect using Affinity Groups:

Identify the Affinity Group: The first step is to identify the Affinity Group of the potential client. This could be based on their industry, hobby, or any other common interest.

By utilizing Affinity Groups, appointment setters can build rapport and create a connection with potential clients, making it easier to set appointments and ultimately drive sales.

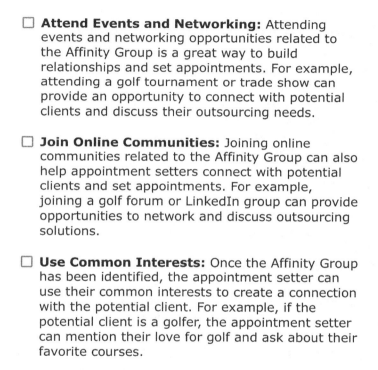

☐ **Attend Events and Networking:** Attending events and networking opportunities related to the Affinity Group is a great way to build relationships and set appointments. For example, attending a golf tournament or trade show can provide an opportunity to connect with potential clients and discuss their outsourcing needs.

☐ **Join Online Communities:** Joining online communities related to the Affinity Group can also help appointment setters connect with potential clients and set appointments. For example, joining a golf forum or LinkedIn group can provide opportunities to network and discuss outsourcing solutions.

☐ **Use Common Interests:** Once the Affinity Group has been identified, the appointment setter can use their common interests to create a connection with the potential client. For example, if the potential client is a golfer, the appointment setter can mention their love for golf and ask about their favorite courses.

I remember connecting with a client over a shared passion for ancient history, which led to a fruitful and long-standing business relationship.

Exercises for Connection Mastery

To cement these principles in practice, I encourage you to:

1. Identify the step in the CAESAR method where you excel and where you can improve, based on what you know.
2. Reflect on a recent connection you made: What worked? What didn't?

Your objective now is to foster a deeper level of understanding and empathy during prospect interactions, leading to stronger connections and increased likelihood of connecting.

Do the following exercise:

Step 1: Make a Call- Reach out to a potential cleint with the intention of establishing a deeper connection. This should not be a "sales call," but rather a relationship-building call (You are still going to attempt to set an appointment, but we want to emphasize the relationship and connection).

Step 2: Pick one area from this chapter you can work on with connecting on your calls: Words, Common Interests, or Affinity groups. If you are not strong in that area, make this your connection point. Meaning If you are using Affinity groups it's time to progress into words. If you are using the attention words, it's time to upgrade to a deeper personal connection in common interests. Remember, you're not trying to "sell anything" at this point. You're just trying to connect on a deeper level.

Step 3: Reflect and Confirm-If you are using words to gain attention ask them if you have their attention for 2 mins. If you are starting at the Affinity Group, Ask them about their connection to that group. If you are connecting deeper with the 12 common interest connectors after they've shared, take a moment to reflect on what you've heard. Then, paraphrase what they've shared back to them to confirm your understanding. This shows that you've truly been listening and that you understand their perspective.

Step 4: Share and Connect- Once they feel heard and understood, share something about yourself or your business that relates to what they've just said. This might be an experience, a challenge you've overcome, or a shared aspiration. Make sure it's genuine and relevant to the conversation.

Step 5: Reflect on the Call- After the call, take a few moments to reflect. Consider the quality of the connection you've made and how well you understood the prospect's perspective.

Step 6: Record and Share- Record your findings and insights from this call. Share your reflections in the group chat for the team to learn from your experience.

Answer the following questions:

1. What language technology in connecting did you attempt?

2. What did you connect around?

3. What was the quality of the connection you established?

4. What could you have done differently to gain an even better connection established?

Let's take a page from Rome's playbook and build our empires, one connection at a time.

Side note for Connection - The Essence of Networking, Affiliations and Establishing Common Interests

Networking is more than exchanging business cards or connecting on social media. It's about building relationships that are mutually beneficial. In my industry real estate, your network is your networth. It's not just about who you know; it's about who knows you and, more importantly, who trusts and respects you to heal pain.

Building a Strong Network: Key Strategies

☐ **Attend Industry Events:** Conferences, seminars, and local meetups are fertile grounds for networking. Be proactive and approachable.

☐ **Offer Value First:** Always think about how you can help others in your network. This approach builds trust and lays a foundation for reciprocity.

☐ **Follow Up and Follow Through:** After meeting someone, follow up with a personalized message. Keep your promises and commitments to earn credibility.

Connecting Case Studies:
Networking Leading to Opportunities

Case Study 1: Strategic Networking and Profitable Partnerships

Background: John had been navigating the competitive real estate investment landscape with moderate success. His focus was on identifying undervalued properties to renovate and flip for a profit. However, he quickly realized that the heart of his business, property renovation, was also his bottleneck due to the lack of a reliable contractor.

The Networking Event: At a local real estate networking event, designed to connect various professionals within the industry, John's path crossed with Mike, a contractor known for his quality work and timely delivery. They struck up a conversation over the hurdles of property renovation. John shared his vision for transforming spaces while maintaining the integrity of the original structures, and Mike contributed insightful tips from his extensive experience. It was a meeting of minds that sparked an immediate connection.

The Partnership: The casual exchange at the event led to a formal sit-down where they discussed the potential for collaboration. Both parties were seeking a trustworthy partner: John needed a skilled contractor who could bring his renovation ideas to life, and Mike was looking for steady, challenging projects that could showcase his craftsmanship.

They agreed to a trial project, renovating a dated bungalow that John had recently acquired. Mike's team worked diligently to execute John's vision, and the result was nothing short of transformative. The bungalow sold quickly, netting a significant profit.

Results: The success of the first project cemented their partnership. They went on to collaborate on multiple properties, each project more ambitious than the last. John's investment acumen combined with Mike's execution expertise proved to be a formidable duo in the real estate market. Together, they not only increased the value of the properties they worked on but also revitalized neighborhoods, contributing to the community's growth.

Conclusion: This partnership highlighted the importance of strategic networking and building relationships within the industry. John's ability to connect and forge a partnership with Mike not only resolved his renovation challenges but also significantly increased his business's profitability and reputation. Their story is a testament to the power of partnerships and the unexpected, profitable alliances that can arise from networking events.

Case Study 2: Cultivating Connections for Leadership Growth

Introduction: Sarah, a seasoned leadership coach with a passion for cultivating the potential in others, recognized the power of community engagement as a means to expand her reach. Her goal was to empower business leaders with the tools and insights necessary to foster strong, dynamic teams and drive organizational success.

The Community Workshop: At a workshop focused on "Innovative Leadership in the 21st Century," held at the local chamber of commerce, Sarah's interactive session on "Emotional Intelligence in Leadership" caught the attention of Alex, a business owner struggling to navigate through a period of high turnover and stagnant growth. Alex was impressed by Sarah's expertise and approachable demeanor, prompting him to inquire about her coaching services.

The Initial Connection: The two engaged in a deep conversation about Alex's business challenges. Sarah's approach to leadership development—centered on authenticity, emotional intelligence, and strategic vision—resonated with Alex. He expressed a need for these elements within his own company, hoping to cultivate a leadership culture that could drive transformation.

The Engagement: Sarah proposed a preliminary consulting engagement, offering to conduct a thorough assessment of the company's leadership dynamics and team structure. Her comprehensive analysis provided Alex with actionable insights, revealing areas for leadership development and team empowerment.

Impressed by her thorough approach and the immediate, positive feedback from his team, Alex secured Sarah's services on a long-term contract. They outlined a series of workshops, one-on-one coaching sessions, and team-building retreats aimed at revamping the company's leadership practices.

Long-Term Impact: Over the course of the year, Sarah's influence permeated the company. Under her guidance, Alex and his team developed a deeper understanding of effective leadership. Morale improved, turnover rates dropped, and productivity soared. The business began to thrive, attributing much of its newfound success to the leadership transformations initiated by Sarah.

Conclusion: Sarah's connection with Alex at the community workshop illustrates the potential of such engagements for generating meaningful business opportunities. Her ability to translate a single workshop interaction into a transformative consulting contract demonstrates the importance of community involvement and the value of targeted, impactful leadership coaching. The business's turnaround served as a powerful case study for Sarah's coaching practice and established her as a sought-after coach in the business community.

Fostering a Sense of Community: Beyond individual connections, being part of a community offers a sense of belonging and support. In real estate, this can mean joining or forming investment groups, participating in online forums, or contributing to local business associations.

John C. Maxwell author of the 21 Irrefutable Laws of leadership says,

> *"A leader is one who knows the way, goes the way, and shows the way."*

There are benefits to building a community & growing in community involvement significantly increase your connection.

☐ **Shared Knowledge and Resources:** In a community, members share insights, experiences, and sometimes even investment opportunities.

☐ **Support and Encouragement:** Growth has it challenges. A community provides moral support and advice.

The journey in growth is enriched through connections. By mastering the idea of connecting around pockets and pools of people through networking and actively participating in communities, you open doors to opportunities that would otherwise remain closed. Remember the Romans built roads?

These roads were really for connection. The focus was on the connection. Connecting markets, economies, and people.

Remember, the strongest connections are built on authenticity, mutual respect, and genuine interest in others' success.

"Whose image is on the coin?" Jesus asks. "Whose inscription?" They reply, "Caesar." Jesus says, "Give to Caesar what is Caesar's, and to God what is God's." (Matthew 22:15-22.)

Ask

(Inquiry is insight – ask and it is given.)

In the journey of growth the ability to 'Ask' is a pivotal skill. You have to ask with intention. This chapter explores how to ask and accelerate your business's growth and navigate the complex landscapes of your market with asking the right question at the right time.

Do not fear asking people direct questions that show your intentions upfront. Before you can formulate your ask you first have to know what your intention is in asking the question. The researchers report in Association for Psychological Science journal "These results suggest that people like question-askers when the questions are directed toward them personally. This further supports the mechanism of responsiveness—we like people who seem responsive to us personally (not to other people in general)((2017, July)."

As I think back to one of my previous training sessions, I remember focusing on the art of inquiry. Did you know one intention question is all you need to set your conversation on the right track, qualify the prospect, and the result of the conversation is always a favorable outcome?

The ask step is a vital tool in the CAESAR Method. "Humans like talking about themselves, so asking questions helps others talk about themselves and will make you seem like a great conversationalist. Obviously, asking questions helps build up new relationships, as it helps to learn more about the other person and what you have in common and creates more understanding (2021, December 3)."

It's not just about asking questions, but about asking the right question, with the right intention. This one pivotal inquiry paves the way for information gathering, engagement, and guiding the client through the CAESAR journey.

There are 7 different intention questions:
1. Setting an Appointment
2. Making a Decision to Become a Client
3. Attend an Event
4. Getting a testimonial or review
5. Recruit talent
6. Delegation
7. Establish a partnership

Dale Carnegie once said, "The art of conversation lies in asking open-ended questions." That simple truth has been a beacon in my practice.

In my experience, asking the right question is like unlocking a door. This door happens to lead to more revenue than you have ever thought possible. It invites a deeper connection and brings the core issues into the open, much like a conflict in a relationship does.

It's in this space, this fertile ground of open dialogue, where true connections are forged and relationships take root. And remember, it's not just about posing the question; it's about listening intently to the answer. This is where trust begins to bloom.

Let's review different types of questions so that we can write our intention question. These are the types of questions that have proven most fruitful in my interactions:

Open-ended questions: These are the seeds of conversation. "Tell me about your experience with our product," or "What challenges are you hoping to overcome?" These inquiries invite a narrative response, giving the soil richness and depth.

Probing questions: Like a farmer assessing the land, we dig deeper. "Can you provide an example of that issue?" or "What specific steps have you taken to address this problem?" These questions unearth the finer details that open-ended questions might miss.

Harvesting Questions: While open-ended questions and probobing questions are intention to sow seeds of benefit for the prospect. Harvesting questions are language technology that allow the prospect to being to align with your interest, and you can begin to harvest from the seeds you have sown in the relationship.

These harvesting questions help your prospect understand that you have placed work into the relationship and they have already received value from you. Here's where we begin to harvest. "Is our solution something you'd consider implementing?" or "When could we schedule a follow-up to discuss about this further?" These inquiries nudge the dialogue toward actionable steps.

In the dance of a sales call, an intention question is the step that leads the conversation with trust. And just like in a dance, the flow of your question can either trip you up or make the experience unforgettable for both parties.

I've learned that an intention question is the bridge to trust. So then how do you do this with out misaliging the potential client and turn them back on the road you are building?

You wouldn't ask for something as personal as a social security number on a first date, right? In the same way, this first critual question you ask in a relationship matters and must build trust incrementally throughout the call.

One more question, when did the relationship with your significant other really start? Was it at the, "Fall in love" stage where everything the other person does or is appears perfect, or did the relationship start at the first conflict?

After we connect, the entire reason that we ask one intention question is to bring the conflict to the forefront of the relationship. This is so we can come to an agreement quickly and continue on with opening the relationship. Understand that the intention here is not to trick people but to be transparent by asking the best question that this is an opportunity to move forward and eventually do business.

I urge you to consider your approach. It's not just a method; it's an art.

The framework for this intention question is:
1. One question
2. Transparent as to the reason for your interaction
3. It must come after your connection, and start your education, while revealing your intention. One of the 7 intentions we discussed earlier.

The following are examples of the three types of questions that I hear being asking all the time and are not the "Ask" step but are connecting or aligning interest question with the prospect:

People Questions - The objective of these questions is to understand the individual you're speaking with and build a connection.

     1. Can you tell me a little bit about your role in the company?

     2. How long have you been in this position?

     3. What drew you to work in this industry?

     4. What do you find most rewarding about your role?

     5. What kinds of challenges are unique to your position?

Productive Questions - These are more general questions about the company, designed to generate conversation about its operations, intentions, and challenges.

     1. Could you tell me a bit about what your company does?

     2. What are some of the major goals your company is currently focusing on?

     3. How does your company differentiate itself in the market?

4. What are some of the challenges your company is facing in achieving its goals?

5. Can you describe your ideal customer?

Personal Questions - These are specific questions about the company, aimed at digging deeper into their operations, culture, or specific issues they're facing.

1. What is your company's strategy for growth this year?

2. How does your team typically handle [specific task or challenge]?

3. How would you describe the company culture here?

4. Are there specific areas where your company is looking for improvements or efficiencies?

5. How do you envision your product/service evolving in the future to meet your customers' needs?

Remember, the key to these questions is not just asking them, but actively listening to the responses and responding in a way that shows understanding and empathy. This is the foundation for building trust.

Asking questions in sales is like fishing. You need to cast your line, wait for a bite, and then reel in your catch. The right questions are like the bait, attracting the attention of your potential client and reeling them in for a successful sale.

Asking an intention question is like filling a trust cup. Just as a cup needs to be filled with liquid to be useful, we need to start our relationships with a question to gather information and create engagement.

The CAESAR method is a proven and effective approach to successfully opening relationships with trust. One of the most critical components of the CAESAR method is this Ask stage, where you have the opportunity to gather information, create engagement, influence them towards your intentions and set the potential client on the track of the CAESAR Method.

> **To set the client on the tracks of the CAESAR method: <u>Ask one power question</u>** right after connecting set the client on the track of the CAESAR method by giving them a roadmap of what to expect. Just like a train conductor guides passengers on a journey, asking one intention question guides the client through the sales process. This helps create a more comfortable and engaging experience for the client and sets them up for a successful outcome.

> > *Example of a power intention question: For BBC Global Services the question we ask has been- What has been your experience using HIPAA Compliant Healthcare Virtual*

Assistants for your staffing.

Example of a power intention question: At Red Maples, LLC. we ask "Are you looking for a property manager?" or "Do you love your current property manager?"

To gather information: Asking this one intention question allows the you to gather information about the client and their needs. This information is critical in determining the best solution for the client and how to effectively communicate the value of your product or service. By gathering information, the you are able to tailor your response to the specific needs of the client and increase the likelihood of a successful outcome.

To get their reason to advance: The client will likely right here bring up the exact reason why they should use your product or service to heal their pain in the form of a brushoff.

To create engagement & trust: Asking questions creates engagement by allowing the client to share their thoughts and concerns. Engagement is key in building relationships and trust with clients. By actively listening to the client and responding to their questions, the appointment setter is able to create a personal connection that sets the stage for a successful appointment.

The thing about asking the exact right question is that it will immediately expose the reason why your potential client will not take action and do the vary thing they need to do to heal their pain.

No money
No time
Existing relationship
Not interested
Can you call me back

These brushoffs are all the exact reasons why these potential clients should move forward but they are holding themselves back. These brushoffs are the same excuse they give to everything in life that they know they should be doing but are standing in their own way.

When it comes to growing your business do you ask the right questions?

What are some questions you should be asking that you are not asking?

Asking is the art of build relationship: Strategic Growth

Facilitation as a Two-Way Street with the company and the facilitator.

The act of 'Asking' is a catalyst for growth. In the realms of real estate and leadership, where challenges are constant and the learning curve is steep, having a Strategic Growth Facilitaor can be a game-changer. Embrace the opportunity to learn from others' experiences as you carve your own path to success.

"Rapid growth isn't magic!"

ASK TRAINING

Welcome to a pivotal session in our CAESAR training series, one that will fine-tune your approach to sales calls: "The Art of Asking Questions."

Picture this: you're on a recent call with a potential client. Now, pause and rewind that scene in your mind. Think about the questions that you peppered throughout the conversation. Were they open-ended, eliciting detailed responses? Or were they probing, designed to dig deeper into a specific area? Maybe they were harvesting questions, those that nudge the conversation towards a decisive action.

Let's take a moment right now. I want you to pull out your notebooks or open a new document on your devices. Go on, I'll wait. I want you to jot down the questions you remember asking.

Classify them: were they open, probing, or harvesting? Now, think critically about how each question served you in that conversation. What did they unveil about your client's needs?

How did they steer the conversation? This reflection is more than an exercise; it's a recalibration of your methods.

As you analyze your questions, consider the CAESAR method's essence—it's about connection, it's about understanding, and ultimately, it's about setting the stage for a successful sale. Your questions are your most powerful tool in this process.

Write out your one power intention question you can use to pivot the connection towards the selling situation.

Remember, the quality of your question can define the caliber of your sales calls. Use them to pave a road to understanding, to align your solutions with your client's pain points, and to guide them to the realization that what you're offering is not just a product or service—it's a pathway to their success.

Now, let's regroup and share. Who would like to volunteer a question they've used and discuss its impact? Don't be shy; this is how we learn—through sharing, through community.

It's in your power to make every call a journey of discovery for your client, and in doing so, lead them to the mutual goal of a successful sale. So, let's master the art of questioning, for it's the heartbeat of the CAESAR method and the lifeline of our sales success. Thank you, and now let's open the floor to discussion and practice.

Educate

Walking into the third phase of our CAESAR journey, we find ourselves in the realm of Education. It's here where we lay the foundation of trust and credibility with our potential clients, distinguishing ourselves from the competition by not just informing, but truly enlightening them about our services, products, and solutions.

Albert Einstein once said,
"The only source of knowledge is experience."

That resonates with me, especially when I think about the time I stepped into a car dealership. I was greeted with enthusiasm, but quickly bombarded with an avalanche of information that left me more lost than when I entered.

Contrast that with a different visit, where a savvy salesperson engaged me with stories that illuminated the cars' features and how they matched my life—stories that turned specs into scenarios I could see myself in. By the end of it, I walked out not just with a car, but with a story I was eager to continue.

A 2022 study by Baylor College of Medicine, published in Science Daily, discovered that oxytocin is generated during learning activities, showing its role in creating neural connections necessary for learning (Baylor College of Medicine, 2022, December 9). This chemical also helps build trust, which is crucial in the CAESAR Method.

In my work, I've seen how powerful storytelling can be. It's not just about sharing information; it's about crafting stories that help people see themselves finding solutions through what we offer. This could be through sharing personal experiences, celebrating client achievements, sharing touching feedback, detailing transformative journeys, or highlighting positive reviews. Each narrative has its unique value.

Whether it's personal anecdotes, client successes, heartfelt testimonials, case studies that map a journey of transformation, or even leveraging the collective voice of satisfied clients through Google reviews, each story serves a purpose.

For instance, when I share the benefits of partnering with Red Maples, our property management business, I am always educating the prospects on how we have increase professionalism, proficiency, and profitability — for our investors, I'm not just listing features. I'm painting a picture of a business where these ***results have healed the pains they had*** and provide our competitive advantage.

I might say something like: *"During our*

consultation, we will discuss your investment portfolio and explore how Red Maples can help you optimize your returns through our management services. We will discuss the 3 financial ratios all small multifamily investors should know, the 11 ways to drive your revenue and a number of way to control costs"

When I talk about the successes of businesses using the CAESAR Method, such as partnering with BBC Global for appointment setting, I highlight more than just the benefits of increased efficiency, cost savings, and better appointment rates.

I explain the real issues it solves, like the struggle U.S. companies face in hiring reliable entry-level employees at reasonable wages, a challenge we've helped hundreds of clients overcome.

This approach helps clients imagine a scenario where their operations are more efficient and their profits are higher. It's not solely about the services we provide; it's about how these services seamlessly integrate into the unique challenges each business faces. Through stories of real-life applications, I show how our appointment setting can simplify a busy calendar or reduce the burden of administrative duties, offering a tailored solution to each client's specific situation.

I consider every educational moment with a client as

sowing a seed. And with the right nurture, tailored education and information, that seed sprouts into a robust, flourishing relationship.

> So here's an exercise I encourage you to embrace: In your next client interactions, bring two different stories to the table. Reflect on them afterward.

> What was the core message?

> Why that particular story?

> What was the impact?

Use these reflections to refine your storytelling, to ensure that with each tale told, you're not just educating, but truly connecting.

To sum up, the art of educating in the CAESAR Method is more than a step in the process—it's a commitment to understanding, a commitment to relationship-building, and a commitment to growth, both for our clients and for ourselves.

At the core of success is the continuous pursuit of education. This Educate step focuses on the 'Educate' aspect of the CAESAR Method, emphasizing the importance of acquiring and updating knowledge in order to educate your clients about things they need to be aware of as to why they need to take the next step. There are three places to do the research for this education information for your organization and they are internally, industry, and instructional materials.

Internal and Tribal Knowledge

- ☐ **Continuous Education:** Influence and growth are not static skills but a dynamic practice that evolves with experience and learning.
- ☐ **Keep Abreast of New Trends:** Company solutions and practices evolve, so it's crucial to stay updated through the data and business trends.
- ☐ **Learn from Company Leaders:** Study the lives and strategies of successful leaders in your company. This can provide practical insights and inspiration. Many leaders can provide these results and stories needed to educate others.
- ☐ **Satisfied Clients:** Gather Google Reviews, Testimonials, and video interviews of satisfied clients. One that tell their pain and your ability to heal that pain.

Industry Knowledge

While the following are specific to the Real Estate Industry, learn to apply them to your specific industry.

- ☐ **Real Estate Knowledge:** It's important to build

your foundation of industry knowledge. The real estate market is complex and ever-changing. Staying educated is key to making informed investment decisions.

☐ **Understand Market Dynamics:** Learn how economic factors, market trends, and regulations affect real estate investment.

☐ **Financial Acumen:** Develop a strong grasp of real estate financing, including loans, mortgages, and tax implications.

☐ **Property Management:** Acquire knowledge in managing properties effectively to enhance their value and profitability.

Educational Resources and Tools

☐ **Books and Publications:** Stay well-read on subjects related to your clients pains and the solutions.

☐ **Online Courses and Workshops:** Engage in continuous learning through various educational platforms offering information about the pain of treatments to that pain

☐ **Networking Events and Conferences:** These can be excellent opportunities for learning from experienced professionals and gain tid bits of information to frame in your education.

It is important to put together, within your company, these training sessions on a regular basis to keep the team learning about the education step in the CAESAR method. Each training you hold provides facts and stories to share and educate your clients as to why they should take the next step with you.

Practical Application: Bridging Knowledge and Action

Education in Strategic Growth Facilitation is not just about gathering information; it's about applying this knowledge practically. Making a company wide commitment to educating the prospects, clients, prospective employees, and employees.

Education is the cornerstone of success in both Strategic Growth Facilitation. Educating someone might help influence them towards your intentions but they will not feel manipulated or deceived. This is when you use only information that is 100% true. By committing to continuous learning and practical application, you equip yourself with the tools necessary to navigate challenges and seize opportunities effectively and provides the prospect an opportunity to agree with your intention and take the next step.

Remember, in the world of Strategic Growth Facilitation, there is always more to learn, and the most successful individuals are those who embrace education as a lifelong journey, keep learning and keep sharing.

"If the last time you trained was in school you are leaving thousands if not millions of dollars on the table."

Set the Intention

(Intention sets the sail.)

Picture this: After a long day of running around, playing, and general kiddo activities, it's finally time for my little girl to settle down for the night. We were snuggled up getting ready for bed, hair wet from a recent shower, cheeks flushed from the last of her tireless energy. It's that special time of day when the world slows down and we get to talk about anything and everything that comes to mind.

In the quiet, my wife decided to ask her, "Did you remember to wash up before bed?" I thought to myself " Her hair is wet and she just took a shower." "Why is my wife asking?" My daughter was 9 years old at this point and was in the shower for like 10 - 15 minutes.

She gives us a tired but cheeky grin, and with all the innocence and candor only a child can muster, she announces proudly, "*I washed my armpits and feet!*"

I couldn't help but chuckle at this. Here I was, expecting a simple 'yes' or 'no', and she gives us this gem. It's moments like these, unexpected and utterly hilarious, that lighten the humdrum of daily routines. And it's a testament to the frankness of children – to them, washing the stinkiest parts equates to total cleanliness.

It makes sense in a way, doesn't it? And the craziest part is she was 9 years old! Come to think of it, I hope she was joking with us.

And so, every time the world gets a little too serious, I think back to my little girl, proudly proclaiming her partial cleanliness, and I'm reminded of the absolute joy and amusement that can be found in the simplest of things, even in armpits and feet.

Just like my little girl had her intention you need you have intention in the conversation with your prospects. Setting clear intentions is crucial for Strategic Growth Facilitation. This chapter explores how setting specific, measurable, and achievable intentions can steer your journey toward success. It's about transforming vision into actionable objectives.

In the pursuit of growth, both personal and professional, I've learned that the power of goal setting is not just in listing desires—it's in defining the path to achieving them. Clarity has become my cornerstone; I ask myself, "What does success actually look like?" Is it steering my team to peak performance, or is it the thrill of closing deal after deal on new properties?

Success for me is tangible. It's not just about having ambitions; it's about making them measurable. I've set targets to amplify my rental income by 15% and to elevate my team's productivity by 20%. These aren't just numbers—they're milestones that mark my journey to strategic growth.

Time is the canvas on which I paint my intentions. It's not enough to say what I want to achieve; I need to specify, "by when?" Assigning realistic timelines breathes life into my intentions infusing them with urgency and making progress tangible. It's the ticking clock that reminds me that every moment is a step towards my aspirations.

Over the years, my strategies for effective goal setting have evolved:

- ☐ **SMART Goals:** Each goal I set is a promise I make to my future self, and the SMART framework is my vow of commitment. Specific, measurable, achievable, relevant, and time-bound—these aren't just adjectives; they're my criteria for success.
- ☐ **Vision Boards:** I've surrounded myself with visual reminders of where I'm headed. Vision boards and mind maps don't just decorate my office; they're the visual echoes of my ambition, keeping my focus razor-sharp.
- ☐ **Action Plans:** Every large goal is a mountain to climb, and I've learned to conquer each by

breaking them down into smaller, actionable steps. This simplification transforms daunting tasks into manageable checkpoints.

☐ **Regular Reviews:** Just as the seasons change, so do the landscapes of our goals. Setting aside regular intervals to review and recalibrate ensures that my strategy is as dynamic as the markets I navigate.

☐ **Accountability:** My goals are not whispered secrets; they're declarations of intent. Sharing them with a mentor or colleague transforms them into commitments etched in reality.

☐ **Celebrate Milestones:** Every small win is a cause for celebration. These moments of acknowledgment are not just pats on the back; they're the fuel that powers my drive towards the next milestone.

The intention setting stage is so important, it is what you want them to do that will ultimately help them in their own intentions. That line is so good I'm going to say it again. "The intention setting stage is so important, it is what you want them to do that will ultimately help them in their own intentions."

Setting the intention in my work has meant defining clear objectives for calls, appointments, presentations, sales, average sales prices, and referrals. For instance, my intention may be to increase my calls by 10% month over month, or to boost my appointment set rate by two additional appointments per week. Perhaps it's about enhancing the quality of presentations to lift my average sales price by 5%, or cultivating relationships that will double my referrals in a quarter.

In essence, setting intention is the art of turning the intangible into the tangible, the ordinary into the extraordinary, and the dreams into reality. It's the art I practice every day, the discipline that shapes my growth, and the commitment that drives my success.

My wife and I even teach our daughter that we don't care what people do, we only care about what they want. We ask her to focus on intention and ignore distractions. Anything that is not the intention is the distraction.

Once you know your intentions you know what area of your process you are going to focus on improving. It is important to know that you potential clients have these intentions too!

Your job is to set the intention to the next step in the relationship at this point in the conversation. Remember people will not take step 2 until they take step one and you must be able to gain a commitment to take the next step in the relationship.

Stepping into am ice cream shop, I'm instantly reminded

of the power of setting an intention that aligns with the prospects intention. It was there, amid the sweet aroma of waffle cones, where I grasped the essence of and power of aligned intentions. "Cone or cup?" the server asked, presenting a choice so effortlessly simple, yet profoundly effective. This is the heart of the 'either or' technique, a technique I've come to rely on in my own practice.

When I'm on a call with someone interested in my service, ready to seal the commitment, I draw from a palette of techniques to set intentions and to make the decision easy for my client. It's about guiding them to a 'yes' they want to say, with the same ease of choosing between a cone or a cup. "Great," I often say,"Would you prefer to schedule our meeting for next Monday at 10 AM, or does Wednesday at 2 PM work better?" *The either or technique*.

Or perhaps I might say the followign to align intentions with the next step, "I have Wednesday at 2 PM set aside for you, okay?" *The assumptive technique*. These techniques, woven seamlessly into the conversation, ease the client into a decision without pressure, respecting their need for flexibility.

Another way of setting intentions is offering a series of choices, a tactic known as the *alternate of choice* , might be your key. "I have availability next Monday,

Tuesday, or Thursday at 2 PM, which day aligns best with your schedule?"

Setting intentions should be as satisfying as savoring your favorite ice cream on a warm summer day. You have an array of flavors at your disposal, an assortment of techniques to sweeten the outcome. The goal is always to find the right match for the client, the flavor that resonates with their palate.

Intention and taking the next step are important in revenue generation. You might need the propset to take the next step and make a choice of the product or service offering or choose how they are going to pay. Don't confuse any step when aligning intention. Make sure that you focus on gaining confirmation of alignment in the exact step you are in without moving ahead or allowing your prospect to think that are further in the process than they are at.

During one of my workshops, I like to bring these techniques to life. Picture me, armed with an ice cream scoop, demonstrating each technique as if scooping out flavors for the client to choose from. This exercise isn't just about memorization; it's about embodying the technique, making it a part of your sales DNA.

To set intentions is to craft the finale of a well-played symphony. Being assumptive is like the crescendo, the either or option is the rhythm that keeps the melody flowing, and the alternate of choice, is the harmony that brings it all together. Each has its place, and when executed with skill, can set the stage for a harmonious relationship.

In the context of the CAESAR method, setting intentions with a prospect is akin to laying down a clear path for a journey you both will embark on together. This approach is grounded in the principle that clarity and mutual understanding from the outset are key to successful outcomes. Here's a simplified way to think about it:

Imagine you're planning a road trip with a friend. Before you even start the engine, you both agree on the destination, the route you'll take, the stops you'll make, and what you hope to experience along the way. Setting intentions in sales is much like planning this trip. It involves discussing with your prospect what you both aim to achieve, how you plan to get there, and what steps you'll take together.

Define the Destination: Start by clearly identifying what your prospect wants to achieve. This could be solving a specific problem, reaching a new goal, or improving their current situation.

Map Out the Route: Once the destination is clear, outline how your service or product can help them get there. This is where you explain the process or steps involved in working with you.

Agree on Milestones: Just like planning stops on a road trip, agree on key milestones or check-ins throughout the process. This ensures you both stay aligned and can adjust the plan as needed.

Set Expectations: Discuss what each of you expects from the other. For the prospect, it might involve time, investment, or actions they need to take. For you, it's about the support and guidance you'll provide.

Confirm the Agreement: Finally, make sure both you and the prospect are in agreement with the plan. This could be a verbal confirmation or a more formal agreement, depending on your process.

By setting intentions using the CAESAR method, you're not just selling a product or service; you're forging a relationship based on clear, mutual intentions. This approach not only helps build trust but also ensures that both parties are committed to the journey ahead, leading to more meaningful and successful outcomes.

For further understanding of the importance of intention in shaping behavior and outcomes, refer to Icek Ajzen's Theory of Planned Behavior, this theory suggests that intention is the most direct and immediate predictor of someones behavior. According to Icek, intention is influenced by attitudes toward the behavior, subjective norms, and perceived behavioral control. Ajzen's work is foundational in understanding the intention-behavior relationship across various contexts (Ajzen, I. (1991). This foundational theory supports the CAESAR method's emphasis on the critical role of setting intentions for achieving desired results.

Imagine this: My daughter, after dinner, doesn't simply ask if we want dessert; she presents a choice between chocolate cake or ice cream. Either way, her intention is set, dessert is served. This simple, yet effective tactic mirrors my strategy in setting intentions. It's not about persuasion; it's about presenting options that naturally lead to the mutually desired outcome.

Do not be afraid of stating, setting, or aligning your intentions with others. In my world of appointments and sales intentions, setting the intention is as critical as choosing the right flavor of ice cream. It's about defining clear, actionable objectives—be it the number of calls I make, the appointments I set, the presentations I deliver, the sales I close, the average price points I aim for, or the referrals I generate. Each intention is a promise to myself, a commitment to the growth.

Remember, the power to secure the next step lies in confidence, persistence, and the ability to present options that lead to your desired outcome. By mastering these techniques, I've not only bolstered my success but also fortified my overall sales strategy. Every next step is a testament to the power of a little extra "umph" in my approach. "Umph" added to intentions equals Triumph.

So my intention is to set an appointment with you to talk about the CAESAR method and how it applies to growing your business: I have a couple spots open at 3 PM on my calendar, or we could do 4:30 PM CST. Which time works better for you?

Training Session:
Mastering the Art of Setting The Intention (An Appointment) with the CAESAR Method

Objective:

Equip participants with effective closing techniques to set appointments confidently and increase conversion rates.

Duration: 90 minutes
Materials Needed:
Notepads and pens for participants
Sample scripts for various closing techniques
Role-play scenarios for practice
Timer for exercises
Presentation slides with key points

Training Outline:

1. Introduction (10 minutes)
Welcome and icebreaker activity. Brief overview of the CAESAR Method's importance in the sales process. Introduce the objective of the session

2. The Power of Choice (10 minutes)
Explain the 'either or' and 'assumptive' techniques with

real-life analogies. Share personal anecdotes of successful outcomes. Emphasize the impact of offering choices on decision-making

3. Techniques Deep Dive (20 minutes)
Discuss different techniques: Assumptive , Either or, and Alternate of Choice. Provide examples for each technique. Highlight the importance of respecting the client's decision-making process.

4. Interactive Demonstration (15 minutes)
Use props to simulate different scenarios. Engage participants in acting out each technique. Facilitate a reflection on which technique felt most natural and why

5. Role-Play Exercise (20 minutes)
Break participants into pairs for role-playing exercises Assign each pair a scenario and a technique. Conduct timed role-plays, followed by group discussions

6. Review and Feedback (10 minutes)
Gather the group for a feedback session on the role-plays Discuss what worked, what didn't, and why Offer constructive feedback and alternative approaches

7. Setting Personal Intentions (5 minutes)
Guide participants to set clear intentions for their marketing, sales calls, appointments, etc Encourage them to write down their specific intentions: number of calls, appointments, etc.

8. Words of Encouragement (5 minutes)

Share motivational insights on the importance of perseverance and confidence in sales
Reiterate the "umph" in triumph analogy for motivation

Directions for Execution:

- [ ] **During Interactive Demonstration:** Hand out the props and explain the context of each technique. Allow volunteers to demonstrate first, then encourage all participants to try.

- [ ] **During Role-Play Exercise:** Set a timer for each role-play scenario to keep the activity dynamic. Ensure participants switch roles to experience both sides of the interaction.

- [ ] **Setting Intention Training:** Encourage participants to commit to applying one new technique in their next sales call. Remind them that practice is key to mastering these techniques.

- [ ] **Post-Training Follow-Up:** Send out the role-play scenarios and a summary of the techniques as a reference. Schedule a follow-up session to discuss real-world applications and gather success stories.

Align Interest

(Alignment is the alchemy of success)

Several years back, I found myself seated at a rehearsal for the musical "Footloose" at Lindenwood University, where I was set to play the drums. It was during this practice that I witnessed an enlightening moment unfold between the conductor, the guitarist, and the violin section. The conductor was emphasizing the importance of harmony in music, contrasting it with the concept of dissonance—a lack of harmony that often results in a sense of tension or clash between notes that don't quite blend.

This musical lesson struck a chord with me, especially when considered in the context of aligning interests with prospects. Just as in music, where harmony brings together different notes to create a pleasing auditory experience, aligning interests in a professional setting involves synchronizing our goals with those of our clients or prospects. This alignment is crucial for creating a smooth, harmonious relationship, rather than one marked by dissonance or conflicting objectives.

If you research the science of harmony, particularly in

the realm of brain waves, offers a fascinating parallel. Research has shown that when people work together in a cooperative and synchronized manner, their brain waves can begin to align. This phenomenon, known as brainwave synchronization or neural entrainment, occurs when individuals engage in activities that necessitate mutual understanding and collaboration. The resulting harmony in brain waves is not just a metaphor but a tangible manifestation of unity and synchrony.

In professional relationships, achieving this kind of harmony means actively listening to our prospects, understanding their needs and challenges, and aligning our solutions accordingly. Just like the conductor guiding the musicians to adjust their pitch, tempo, and dynamics to achieve a harmonious performance, we must guide our interactions with prospects with empathy, flexibility, and a genuine desire to meet their needs.

The lesson from that rehearsal at Lindenwood University extends beyond the musical domain, illustrating a universal truth: whether in music or in business, harmony arises from a deep understanding, respect, and alignment of interests. By applying the principles of harmony to our professional interactions, we can create relationships that are not only successful but also resonate on a deeper, more meaningful level.

Just as dissonance in music calls for resolution, any misalignment in our professional engagements beckons for a re-tuning of our approach to ensure that we are in sync with our prospects. The goal is to create a symphony of cooperation that benefits all parties involved, driven by the underlying science of harmony that binds us together, both in music and in life.

Qualification is exclusive, alignment is inclusive. Stop excluding people from buying from you. Alignment of interests is essential in both marketing and sales efforts. This chapter focuses on aligning your personal and professional intentions with those of your stakeholders, whether they are team members, clients, or investors. It's about creating a synergy where everyone's intentions contribute to mutual success.

Have the courage to ask others about their interest. Do not fear the possibility of rejection. In the CAESAR method, the 2nd "A" symbolizes a cornerstone concept: Align Interest.

My role here is to forge a path where my client's pain points and the services I offer converge, creating a relationship that's mutually beneficial. To accomplish this, I make it my mission to deeply understand the specific pain points and interests of my clients.

Abraham Lincoln said, "The best way to predict the future is to create it." This resonates with me profoundly. As I envision myself as a gardener tending to an array of plants, each with distinct preferences for soil, water, and sunlight, I apply the same care and attention to nurturing my client relationships. I invest time to learn about their current landscape, their targets for growth, and the hurdles they're facing. Armed with this knowledge, I am well-equipped to propose solutions that are not just effective but perfectly suited to their unique environment.

In my practice, aligning a client's interests requires a thoughtful approach. It's akin to having a keyring with an array of keys, each representing a different service or solution, and discerning which key fits their lock. The better I understand their pain, the more precise I become in selecting the right key, unlocking opportunities for both of us.

I often engage in role-play exercises where it's kinda like being a doctor. We need to understand the cause or the pain that will allow for the right treatment plan. This role-play with my colleagues is designed to sharpen this skill. We alternate between playing the roles of client and salesperson, immersing ourselves in the process of discovery and alignment. This not only improves our ability to connect with clients but also enhances our proficiency in finding the perfect treatment plan.

The 2nd "A" in my CAESAR method is more than a step; it's a philosophy that underpins my entire approach to sales and client relationships. By aligning interests, I don't just aim for successful transactions; I strive for relationships where connection is the currency and value is recognized. Through this process, I don't just look to meet expectations, I aim to exceed them, crafting relief to their pain alongside my clients that we've both had a hand in creating.

In crafting a script that engages potential clients and sets the stage for a successful business evaluation, it's crucial to integrate key questions that not only demonstrate your understanding of their pain but also pave the way for an effective relationship. Here's a framework to creating such a script, tailored to resonate with any client across various industries.

- ☐ **Slight Take-away:** Begin by establishing the context for the client's commitment, subtly reminding them that this process is an opportunity that might not always be readily available. This instills a sense of value for your service.
- ☐ **Probing for Pain Points:** Ask targeted questions to uncover the pain your client faces. Your aim is to not only identify these issues but also to encourage the client to acknowledge their need for a solution. It's critical you do not offer the

solution here you simply keep asking about this pain. I like to say when training we need 2 yeses to pain admission and we need to understand the emotional impact before moving on in the process.

- ☐ **Confirmation:** Reaffirm the next steps they have already agreed to, review the details to ensure both parties are in sync. Gain a commitment with harvesting question to following the next steps.

- ☐ **Cultivating the Need:** Encourage the client to think critically about their current pain. Between steps. This self-reflection primes them for a more in-depth conversation during your next meeting.

- ☐ **Building a History:** Understanding the client's past attempts at solutions or previous partnerships can offer invaluable context for how to serve them effectively.

- ☐ **Detail Confirmation:** Ensure the client has all necessary information at hand to prevent any confusion or miscommunication. Have them write it down, enter it in their calendar, or simply say back to you the details to ensure they understand.

- ☐ **Involving Decision-Makers:** Stress the importance of having all relevant parties present during the next step to facilitate a comprehensive discussion and decision-making process.

Example Script from BBC Global Services:

Note: This script has been modified to protect their privacy and script we created together.

"As we prepare for our appointment on Friday at 9am, It's important to have a clear picture of where you stand currently, so we are going to ask you some questions to ensure we are not going to be wasting anybodys time, Okay:

What have you done historically to try and fill your open roles?

If we were to ask your staff about thier current workload what would they say about the volume of work they have?

What benchmarks do you employ to gauge success in your for your employees?

Are there any regulatory standards specific to your industry that we should be aware of?

If you've engaged with outsourcing partners before, what was that experience like for you?"

After these questions, gently guide the client to consider the upcoming meeting: "As we approach our scheduled business evaluation on [Insert Date and Time], I encourage you to reflect on the aspects of your pain points and emotions that are most pressing. This introspection is key to a productive dialogue.

Furthermore, could you ensure you have the following details on hand? It's important we're both fully prepared:

The name and contact information of our respective companies

The specifics of our scheduled conversation

Any relevant documents or background information that could inform our discussion

Lastly, who is the person in your business that would be involved in this decision? Their insights could prove invaluable. And before we conclude, may I ask if can be there?

Lastly, is there anything that could potentially prevent our appointment?"

This comprehensive script framework, when personalized, can be a powerful tool in setting the stage for a successful client engagement and laying the groundwork for a relationship built on understanding and results.

Understanding Stakeholder Interests

- [ ] **Identify Your Stakeholders:** In real estate, this could be investors, tenants, or business partners. In leadership, it could be your team, superiors, or shareholders.
- [ ] **Understand Their Needs and intentions:** Engage in conversations to understand what your stakeholders seek to achieve. This could range from financial returns to job satisfaction.
- [ ] **Align with Your Intentions:** Find common ground where your intentions and your stakeholders' intentions intersect.
- [ ] **Communication:** Maintain open, transparent, and frequent communication. This builds trust and ensures everyone is on the same page.
- [ ] **Collaborative Planning:** Involve stakeholders in the planning process. This fosters a sense of ownership and alignment.
- [ ] **Alignment of Solutions:** Aim for solutions that benefit all parties. In negotiations, look for outcomes that satisfy everyone's core interests.
- [ ] **Identify Potential Conflicts:** Be proactive in identifying where interests might clash.
- [ ] **Open Dialogue:** Address conflicts through open and honest discussions.

Aligning interests is crucial for sustained success and

harmony in strategic growth. It's about understanding what drives others and finding ways to integrate those drivers with your own goals. When interests are aligned, efforts are magnified, conflicts are reduced, and outcomes are more impactful. Remember, true alignment is a continuous process of engagement, understanding, and adjustment, ensuring that all parties move forward together.

Control and manipulation are not selling. There is no influence in these concepts. Selling is influence that is an alignment of interestes. When people have pain they are motivated to pay a price to have the pain healed. They need to know you have the treatment and your organization is competent to provide the treatment plan for them. Deceit and any step in the process destroys trust.

Referrals

(Referrals are the echoes of excellent service – they carry your reputation further than you could ever go alone.)

Welcome to the final stage of the CAESAR Method - Referrals. As the saying goes, "A referral is the greatest compliment a business can receive." It is a testament to the quality of our services and the satisfaction of our clients. In this session, we will delve into how to ask for referrals in an effective and professional manner.

I want to share a story that not only encapsulates the essence of this lesson we are about to explore but also serves as a testament to the power of genuine connections and generosity. It was a typical afternoon, with the sun casting a warm glow through my office window, when my phone rang. It was my friend Jason on the other end, his voice crackling with excitement. "You won't believe how much my business has grown!" he exclaimed, barely able to contain his enthusiasm.

As the conversation continued, it became clear that Jason's success was not just a stroke of luck. He revealed that over 70% of his revenue could be traced back to our relationship. This revelation was both humbling and profoundly illuminating. It underscored a principle that had been a cornerstone of my philosophy:

the power of giving referrals.

This story with Jason isn't just about the success of one business or the impact of one relationship. It's a broader narrative on the cyclical nature of generosity and the profound effects it can have on our lives and the lives of those around us. To receive referrals, you must first be willing to give them. This principle is simple, yet it embodies a depth of truth about human interactions and professional networks.

Are you a giver or taker?

But how does one become a person who gives referrals, you might ask? It starts with a mindset of abundance rather than scarcity. It's about looking beyond immediate gains and fostering relationships with a genuine desire to help others succeed. When you operate from this place of generosity, you create a ripple effect. You not only contribute to others' success but also set the stage for reciprocal generosity. This is not a strategy for the impatient; it requires time, sincerity, and an authentic commitment to the well-being of your network, following the CAESAR method in every relationship.

Jason's story is a vivid illustration of this principle in action. Our relationship, built on mutual support and genuine interest in each other's success, had catalyzed a significant portion of his business growth. This wasn't a transactional exchange but a natural outcome of a culture of generosity.

Jason's story serves as a powerful reminder of the values that underpin lasting success. In a world that often emphasizes competition and self-interest, the art of giving referrals stands out as a beacon of collaborative success. It's a testament to the idea that our success is inextricably linked to the success of those around us.

So, remember the story of Jason. Let it inspire you to be a conduit of opportunity for others, to cultivate relationships with generosity at their core, and to build a legacy defined not just by what you achieve, but by how you uplift others along the way. In doing so, you'll discover that the richest rewards come not from the referrals you receive, but from those you give.

A famous quote that perfectly encapsulates the essence of referrals is by Maya Angelou, who said, "People will forget what you said, people will forget what you did, but people will never forget how you made them feel." This highlights the importance of creating a positive experience for your clients, as they will be more likely to refer others to you if they have had a good experience with you.

The key to growing our business through referrals is to provide excellent service and create a positive experience for our clients. By doing so, we can earn their trust and they will be more likely to refer others to us. One of the steps I find that most people are afraid to follow through on is the referral step. It is critical to not be afraid and ask for the referral.

When asking for referrals, there are a few different approaches we can take. One approach is to simply ask if they know anyone who may be in need of our services.

The R in CAESAR stands for Referrals, and asking for referrals is a critical component of any successful sales process. It's important to understand that referrals do more than just bring in new business. They also help build trust with potential clients by demonstrating that you're confident enough in your services to share them with others.

Incorporating the power of referrals into your sales process can significantly enhance its effectiveness. Let me explain three pivotal ways in which asking for referrals can transform your approach:

Building Trust: Transparency is key in any business relationship, and by soliciting referrals, you signal a level of openness about your services. This openness is not just about showcasing the quality of what you offer; it's an invitation for others to validate and vouch for your services. It's a statement that you believe so strongly in

123

the value you provide that you're willing to have it scrutinized by others. This willingness to be evaluated by your clients' peers fosters a deep sense of trust.

Initiating Conversations: Asking for referrals naturally prompts potential clients to contemplate your services in relation to their needs and those of their acquaintances. This contemplation can lead to a realization of the universal applicability of your services, whether they consider themselves unique in their needs or part of a larger demographic in search of outsourcing solutions. In essence, the mere act of asking for referrals gets people thinking about your services in a more engaged and personal way.

Generating New Business: Ultimately, the aim of seeking referrals is to expand your client base. When a potential client provides a referral, it's an endorsement that places you a step closer to a new sale. This isn't just about numbers; it's about creating a network of mutually beneficial relationships that grow organically from the trust and satisfaction of your existing clients.

Intriguingly, this concept of building trust and community aligns with findings from the Greater Good Science Center, where research by Jeremy Adam Smith (2013) reveals how oxytocin can influence social behaviors. Participants in studies influenced by oxytocin tended to align with the collective decisions of their group, demonstrating the hormone's role in fostering group cohesion and trust. This biological insight underscores the importance of creating a sense of belonging and trust within your client base, enhancing the likelihood of receiving valuable referrals. By understanding these dynamics, you can harness the natural human inclination towards trust and community, leveraging it to bolster your sales strategy effectively.

So, how can you effectively ask for referrals? One technique is to use the "Either/Or Technique" This involves presenting two options and asking the potential client to choose between them. For example, you might say, "Either you can refer me to someone who could benefit from our services, or you can give me the name of someone you know who's already using a competitor's services. Which one would you prefer?"

Another technique is the "Alternate of Choice." This involves presenting two options and asking the potential client to choose between them. Imagine you're in a conversation with a client, and you want to gauge their likelihood of recommending your services. You might say, "On a scale from 1 to 10, with 1 being not likely at all and 10 being highly likely, how likely are you to recommend our services to someone in need?"

Should your client indicate a high likelihood of recommendation, say a 9 or 10, it's the perfect moment to introduce the alternate of choice strategy, which is designed to not only affirm their willingness but also to guide them towards actionable steps they can comfortably take.

You could then articulate the options with persuasive clarity: "That's fantastic to hear, and we're truly grateful for your support. It seems you recognize the value we provide. To help spread the word, we offer a few easy ways for you to share your positive experience. Here are three options for you to consider:

Leave us a Google Review: A quick and effective way to share your satisfaction with our services with others.

Record a Video Testimonial: Your chance to personally express the benefits of our services on camera, giving a face to the testimonial.

Provide a Direct Referral: If there's someone specific you have in mind who could benefit from our services, we'd be honored if you could share their contact information with us.

Which of these options feels most comfortable for you?"

If they opt for the first or second choice, commend their decision and add, "Thank you for taking the time to share your positive experience. Once you've done that, would you be open to us sharing your testimonial with someone you think might benefit from our services? It's a great way to extend your impact and help others discover how they too can benefit."

This method does more than ask for a referral; it provides a structured choice that respects the client's preference and comfort level. It's about making the act of referring as easy and rewarding as possible, thereby turning satisfied clients into active advocates for your business. This approach not only fosters stronger relationships but also enhances the likelihood of generating new business through a foundation of trust and mutual benefit.

It is important to make sure we ask for referrals in a professional and non-invasive manner. We do not want to come across as pushy or insincere. Rather, we want to show our gratitude for their business and ask if they know anyone who may also benefit from our services.

Let's do a quick exercise. Type out your script on how you are currently asking for referrals. I want you to make one appointment with a potential client and attempted to ask for the referral using that script.

Referrals are an invaluable way to grow our business and provide excellent service to even more clients. By asking for referrals in a professional and positive manner, you can expand your reach and continue to provide the best service possible. So, there you have it -

the R in C.A.E.S.A.R. and the power of referrals. Remember, referrals can help build trust, start a conversation, and bring in new business.

Thank you for your attention and I hope this session has been helpful.

In Strategic Growth Facilitation, referrals are a vital component of growth and success. This chapter explores how to cultivate a network and reputation that naturally generate referrals, enhancing your professional reach and impact.

Quick and Final Notes About The Importance of Referrals:

Credibility and Trust: Referrals come with built-in trust, as they are often based on the recommender's positive experiences with you.

Cost-Effective Growth: Acquiring clients or opportunities through referrals is typically more cost-effective than through traditional marketing.

Enhanced Reputation: A steady stream of referrals indicates a strong reputation and high level of satisfaction among your clients or colleagues.

Building a Referral-Generating System

Deliver Exceptional Service: Consistently exceed

expectations in your real estate ventures and leadership roles. Outstanding service leads to word-of-mouth referrals.

Foster Strong Relationships: Build genuine, long-lasting relationships with your clients, colleagues, and network. People refer those they know, like, and trust.

Ask for Referrals: Don't shy away from directly asking satisfied clients or peers for referrals. Ensure it's done tactfully and at an appropriate time.

Leveraging Networking for Referrals

Stay Active in Professional Circles: Regularly engage in industry events, online forums, and community groups related to real estate and leadership.

Follow-Up: Maintain contact with your network. Regular check-ins can keep you top-of-mind.

Offer Reciprocal Referrals: Whenever possible, refer your contacts to others. This reciprocity can encourage them to return the favor.

Nurturing a Referral Mindset

Be Referral-Worthy: Continuously strive to be the best in your field. Excellence breeds referrals.

Communicate Your Appreciation: Always express gratitude for referrals. This can reinforce and encourage ongoing referral behavior.

Track and Analyze Referrals: Keep track of where referrals are coming from to understand which relationships and strategies are most effective.

Referrals are a powerful tool in the arsenal of a successful leader and real estate professional. By focusing on building strong relationships, providing exceptional service, and actively engaging in your professional community, you can create a network that continuously fuels your growth. Remember, a referral-based approach is centered on trust and value continually nurture these, and your network will become one of your greatest assets.

A Brief Exercise:

Now that you've journeyed through the insights and strategies of the CAESAR method, it's time to put your knowledge into action with a straightforward exercise designed to leverage your network for referrals. This exercise isn't just about gaining new leads; it's about strengthening your relationships and helping others along the way. Let's begin:

Step 1: Identify Key Contacts - Start by writing down the names of three business owners you know well and feel closely connected to.

These should be individuals with whom you share a strong, mutual respect.

Step 2: Reflect on Your Connections- Next to each name, jot down how you know each person. Is it through a professional organization, personal friendship, or a past business venture? Then, consider why they might be inclined to refer business to you. What value have you provided to them, or what mutual interests do you share?

Step 3: Craft Your Message- It's time to reach out, but with a twist. Draft an email to these individuals, sharing your discovery of an "incredible new book called the CAESAR method" that you believe could benefit their business growth. If you've purchased the book for them, mention this generous offer; if not, include a link where they can buy the book. This gesture shows you're thinking of their success, not just your own.

Step 4: Implement the CAESAR Method- In your email, apply the CAESAR method to frame your request for referrals. This might look something like demonstrating your understanding of their business challenges, showing empathy, and then suggesting how the CAESAR method (and by extension, your services) could help address these challenges. Conclude by asking if they know anyone who might benefit from similar insights and assistance, thus directly asking for referrals.

Example Email Template:

Subject: A Game-Changing Resource for Business Growth

Dear [Name],

As someone who has always admired your approach to business, I wanted to share something that has truly made a difference in how I view growth and success. I recently came across a book titled "The CAESAR Method," which offers remarkable insights into leveraging personal and professional networks for growth.

I found its approach both innovative and practical, and I couldn't help but think of how it might benefit you as well. [If you bought the book for them, include:] I've sent you a copy as a token of my appreciation for our relationship and in the hope that it offers you as much value as it has to me.

[If you haven't bought the book for them, include:] You can check out the book here [include link]. I truly believe it's worth a read.

In line with the spirit of the CAESAR method, and knowing how much we've both valued our professional exchange of ideas and support, I was wondering if you might know anyone else that is in the (Traget Industry) who could benefit from this book and the growth it promises. Your referral would mean a lot to me, and more importantly, it could significantly aid someone in their business journey.

Thank you for considering this, and regardless, I'd love to catch up soon and hear your thoughts on the book!

Best,

Why This Exercise Matters: This exercise does more than help you ask for referrals; it embodies the essence of the CAESAR method by fostering genuine connections, providing value first, and approaching your network with a mindset of mutual growth. By taking this step, you're not just seeking to expand your business—you're offering a resource that could empower others in their endeavors.

So, take this moment to initiate a cycle of growth, referrals, and strengthened relationships. The power of the CAESAR method isn't just in reading about it; it's in living it.

Brushoffs Vs. Objections

*(In the dance of building relationships,
brushoffs are the off-beats & objections the rhythm
– learn to move to the beat of both.)*

To thrive with the CAESAR method, resilience is not optional, it's fundamental. It's about having a mindset that sees beyond the immediate 'not interested' to the potential 'yes' around the corner.

In my early days of sales, the weight of rejection was a shroud that dimmed the excitement. Daily, I grappled with brush-offs and objections, feeling each 'no time, no money, not interested' chiped away at my resolve. I was green, unseasoned by the relentless cycle of sales, and my numbers, unforgiving as they were, reflected my struggle.

Acknowledgment from my manager became a turning point. It was suggested that resilience, not just persistence, was the key. Thus began my journey towards a mindset that welcomed rejection, not as failure, but as the opportunity.

Once, there was a writer who was paralyzed by the fear of rejection, his manuscripts were gathering dust. One day, he realized that the fear itself was a sign he cared deeply about his work, and this passion was exactly why he needed to brave the submissions. With a deep breath, he sent his stories into the world. His fear, once a barrier, became the reason to move forward, transforming into the courage that landed his first published piece.

Understanding this writers "reasons" for not moving forward may just be the key to improving your opportunity for relationship with more potential customers or clients.

The Art of Handling Brush-offs

A few years ago, I had a rental property that got hit by a tornado.

It was a chaotic scene, with the electricity completely out in the neighborhood. I knew the power was disconnected because I saw the electric meter torn away from the house.

But even in that situation, as I walked through the rooms, I found myself instinctively reaching for the light switches, expecting the lights to miraculously turn on.

This experience taught me a valuable lesson about seeking power in times of conflict or adversity.

Just like I needed electricity to brighten up the dark rooms, we all need a power source to navigate through challenging situations.

When you find yourself in the midst of conflict, whether it's a disagreement, discord, hatred, or any other form of division, remember to tap into your power source. This source brings you the energy and strength to persevere.

It lights you up from within and fuels your determination to keep going. You need a power source that ignites your spirit and empowers you to overcome anything that comes your way.

Peace is not found by avoiding conflict, but by finding power and strength within yourself to face it head-on. Look for that power source that can guide you through any storm and lead you to a place of peace and resolution.

So, when you're facing challenges, remember to connect to your power source, harness your inner strength, and let it guide you toward the peace and strength you desire.

Let your power source be the driving force that lights up

your path and helps you navigate through any situation. When it comes to getting brushed off the phone you can ensure you pluged the potential clients back into the power source if you are not afraid of actually handling the conflict.

The realization that not every negative response is an objection was transformative. Brush-offs are mere diversions, surface-level dismissals that can be navigated with tact and finesse. When someone is trying to brush you off what they are actually doing is saying they don't want the power in their lives turned on right now.

Brushoffs are not objections. They typically come before you 1st attempt to set the intention in the CAESAR Method. Brushoffs are the client in the dark not knowing where to plug in. They think briefly to themselves that you may not possess the power to brighten their day.

Clients are not giving you an objection until they have had the opportunity to be educated about what it is that your organiation does, or the pain you have healed for others.

You might hear things like "I'm not interested," or "I dont have time to deal with this right now" or "I already have a supplier." They are choosing to stay in the dark with this language and using some simple language technology you can turn on the lights long enough for them to have a better understanding of why you are tying to make the connection.

I honed the three following language technologies.

'I understand and...',

'That's exactly why...', and

'Feel, Felt, Found' techniques to turn these moments into opportunities for dialogue and education about our products or services.

It might sound like the following

"I understand that you are not interested and..."

Or

"Being too busy is exactly why I am calling you..."

Or

"I can appreciate how you feel having a supplier you love, many of our clients have felt the same way, here is what they found out..."

Remember back to when you first fell in love for the first time. Did you really have a relationship when everything was going perfect, or did it become a relationship with the first adversity that arose and you came to common ground?

Brushoffs happen very early and it's up to you to care enough about the relationship to be prepared, trained and able to find this common ground with the client. This first brushoff is not really a denial at the relationship but a conflict that skill CAESAR method professionals must help turn on the lights and find common ground.

You are dealing with a brush off if you have not set the intention yet. Use your education to help you get to your intentions.

The Objection as a Gateway

Objections are the client that are out of alignment with you. True objections are not barriers but rather gateways to deeper understanding and a potential long term relationship. Once you have attempted to set the intention you are in a position to see, hear, and work with the client on their objections and mis alignment with your interestes. Objections are perceived barriers to them moving ahead with your intention.

Objections are the problem, A.I.O.A is the solution. Objections signify genuine interest masked as concerns. This is where the A.I.O.A (Agree, Isolate, Overcome, Ask Again) framework shines, it's a structured approach to align interests, provide additional education, and invite further to set the intention.

In Practice

When faced with the classic 'I don't have time for this call,' my response evolved to an understanding acknowledgment, followed by a concise showcase of our service's time-saving benefits from a recent testimonial provided by one of my clients. For the 'I'm not interested'

With genuine objections, such as concerns about service fit, I learned to agree with the client's concerns, validate their feelings. 'Your concern about [objection] is the same concern I was thinking about, it might not be a good fit. Other than [objection] is there any other reason why you would not use our [pain healing solution]. Let me explain how...' and that is why you should make the same decision that 100's of others clients have made and pick a date that works best for you. I have XYZ or ABC.

Resilience in sales is about truly understanding alignment, alignment of mindset, of approach, of self. It's about learning to distinguish between the harmless brush-offs and the substantive objections, each requiring a different key from the salesperson's ring. With patience, practice, and a positive outlook, the once daunting landscape of sales became a ground of endless potential, where each 'no' edged me closer to the 'yes' that mattered. Here are several strategies I adopted:

- [ ] **Normalize Rejection:** Understanding that rejection is not personal freed me from the burden of self-doubt. It's a natural element of the sales process, as common as the changing of seasons.
- [ ] **Learn from Every 'No':** Each rejection holds a lesson. I began to dissect conversations, pinpointing where engagement waned and crafting strategies for improvement.
- [ ] **Cultivate Positivity:** Keeping a positive attitude in the face of adversity propelled me forward. Successes, no matter how small, were my beacons of progress.
- [ ] **Organize and Focus:** Tracking appointments and leads brought clarity and control, essentials for maintaining motivation in a tumultuous landscape.
- [ ] **Realistic Goals:** Setting achievable targets helped me build momentum, celebrate incremental victories, and maintain focus.
- [ ] **Self-Care:** Balancing work with personal time, practicing mindfulness, and seeking mentorship created a foundation strong enough to withstand the rigors of sales.

In the dance of brush-offs versus objections, resilience isn't just part of the choreography; it's the very stage we perform on. The brush-offs, those fleeting shadows that flicker across our path, are simply the unlit corners where opportunity lies in wait. They are not the dead-ends they masquerade as but rather the dimly lit hallways leading us to the auditorium of success. The key to unlocking this is realizing that every brush-off is a silent plea for enlightenment, a client's unconscious beckoning for the light we possess.

Remember that objections, on the other hand, are the open doors beckoning us to connect in the relationship, and you are now armed with our A.I.O.A framework. It is here that the true dance begins asking again leads us through a tango of trust and commitment.

Let's carry with us the mentality that a 'no' is not a finale but a prelude, a prologue to a 'yes' crafted through understanding, patience, and strategic communication. So, as we step off this page and into the field, let's take with us the lessons of resilience, the art of conversation, and the steadfast belief that in the symphony of growth, every note, whether sharp or flat, composes the melody of success.

The MAGIC of MASTERY is not in what you tell people about what you can do, but WHO YOU ARE on the inside!

Application and Adaptation

The CAESAR Method involves the practical application of the principles you've learned and adapting them to your unique circumstances in Strategic Growth Facilitation. This is now about turning theory into action and ensuring that these principles work effectively in your specific context.

How are you going to apply the CAESAR Method in your organzation?

Once there was an appointment setter named Nathan, who lived in the bustling town of Saint Louis, MO. Nathan's role was akin to that of a navigator, charting courses through the tumultuous seas of scheduling and client management. Nathan discovered a scroll of ancient wisdom known as the CAESAR Method, which promised to guide any willing learner through the art of securing commitments, aligning interests, and fostering relationships.

Every morning, amidst the hum of the awakening town, Nathan would reflect on the principles of CAESAR, weaving them into the tapestry of daily conversations. The scroll was not a rigid rulebook but a map, adaptable to the unique rhythm of each day's challenges.

Saint Louis, Mo like any market, was a living entity that shifted with the moods of the economy and the needs of its inhabitants. Nathan, with the CAESAR Method in mind, adapted strategies to meet these ever-changing conditions. When the town was hit by a downturn, Nathan saw an opportunity to refine approaches, ensuring that the principles of CAESAR were the foundation upon which flexibility was built.

Though strategies would shift like the winds, Nathan's core values were unwavering, a constant beacon for clients and colleagues alike. The spirit of CAESAR encouraged Nathan to experiment, to innovate within the space of conversation and connection, trusting that this approach would lead to meaningful appointments and lasting engagements.

Challenges were as common as the calls Nathan made, each one a chance to grow and refine the art of dialogue. Armed with a toolkit of problem-solving techniques and a mindset primed for resilience, Nathan transformed potential rejections into opportunities for learning and connection.

With each interaction, Nathan set clear SMART goals, personal benchmarks of success that went beyond the number of appointments set. These goals were the guiding stars, the personal metrics that shaped a unique path to achievement within the framework of the

CAESAR Method.

As days turned into months, Nathan's journey became a testament to the power of personalization and continuous improvement. The CAESAR Method, once a mere set of guidelines, had become the heartbeat of Nathan's daily practice, the secret sauce to turning prospects into partners.

To those who inquired about the secret to a successful appointment setting, Nathan would often say with a knowing smile, "Embrace the CAESAR within, for it is in the daily practice and the courage to adapt that we find our true path to success." And thus, in the heart of Saint Louis, Nathan's story became a beacon of hope and strategy for all who sought to master the art of appointment setting.

James 2:26 (NIV):

"For as the body without the spirit is dead, so faith without works is dead also."

This verse succinctly captures the synergy between belief (faith) and action (works), mirroring the dynamic relationship between understanding the principles of the CAESAR Method and actively applying them in one's organization. Just as faith is made complete by what one does, the efficacy of the CAESAR Method is realized through its practical application and the willingness to adapt its principles to meet the unique challenges and opportunities that arise in the market.

Integration into Daily Practices

Incorporate the CAESAR principles into your daily routines, decision-making processes, and strategic planning in both leadership roles and real estate activities.

Tailoring to Your Needs: Customize the approach to suit your unique challenges and goals. The CAESAR Method is a framework, not a one-size-fits-all solution.

Adapting to Changing Circumstances

Flexibility: Be prepared to modify your strategies as market conditions, team dynamics, and personal goals evolve.

Continuous Learning and Improvement: Stay open to new information and feedback. Use these insights to refine your approach.

Balancing Consistency with Adaptability

Consistency in Core Values: While tactics and strategies may change, your core values and principles should remain constant.

Experimentation: Don't be afraid to try new approaches. Some of the best strategies come from experimentation and adaptation.

Overcoming Challenges and Setbacks

Resilience: Learn to view challenges as opportunities for growth and improvement.

Problem-Solving Strategies: Develop a toolkit of problem-solving techniques that can be applied in various situations.

Measuring Success and Making Adjustments

Define Metrics for Success: Establish clear metrics to evaluate the effectiveness of the CAESAR Method in your endeavors.

Regular Review and Adjustment: Periodically assess your progress and make necessary adjustments to stay aligned with your goals.

The application and adaptation of the CAESAR Method mark the beginning of a dynamic and continuous journey in Strategic Growth Facilitation. By applying these principles, remaining adaptable, and continuously seeking improvement, you can achieve sustained success and fulfillment in your professional and personal life. Remember, the true power of the CAESAR Method lies in its practical application and your ability to tailor it to your unique journey.

Enjoy!

Pave your path with the CAESAR Method: Transform obstacles into highways to success!

References

1. Association for Psychological Science. (2017, July 14). Asking questions increases likability. Psychological Science in the Public Interest. Retrieved from https://www.psychologicalscience.org/news/minds-business/asking-questions-increases-likability.html
2. Ajzen, I. (1991). The theory of planned behavior. Organizational Behavior and Human Decision Processes, 50(2), 179-211.
3. Baylor College of Medicine. (2022, December 9). Oxytocin drives development of neural connections in adult-born neurons, study finds. ScienceDaily. Retrieved from https://www.sciencedaily.com/releases/2022/12/221208174229.htm
4. Oblivious?. (2021, December 3). How does asking questions help create closer relationships? Retrieved from https://www.areweoblivious.com/de/blogs/news/how-does-asking-questions-help-create-closer-relationships
5. Smith, J. A. (2013, October 17). Five surprising ways oxytocin shapes your social life. Greater

Good Magazine. Greater Good Science Center. Retrieved from https://greatergood.berkeley.edu/article/item/five_ways_oxytocin_might_shape_your_social_life

6. Zak, P. J. (2017). The neuroscience of trust: Management behaviors that foster employee engagement. Harvard Business Review, (January–February 2017). Retrieved from https://hbr.org/2017/01/the-neuroscience-of-trust

About the Author:

Nathan Bush is a dynamic speaker, insightful author, and the creative force behind successful ventures like The Coin System™, Launch Masters International, and Red Maples, LLC. Holding an MBA with an accounting emphasis from Keller Graduate School and a B.A. in Nonprofit Management from Lindenwood University, Nathan has carved a niche for himself in marketing and property management. He shines as a national speaker and workshop facilitator, covering diverse topics from personal development to The CAESAR Method.

Nathan's YouTube channel, Mind Renovation Nation, is where he shares transformative insights and strategies. His prowess in driving change and fostering growth is underscored by his book *Leadership Coaching as a Strategy for Employee Development* and a proven track record of enhancing company culture, customer and colleague retention, and operational efficiency.

For more info visit: linktr.ee/nathanbushmba

Nathan's expertise not only in real estate & property management but also in executing strategic growth initiatives makes him an invaluable resource for those looking to scale their operations and achieve exceptional results.

Hire Nathan to Speak:
NATHAN BUSH, MBA: Catalyst for Growth, Team Inspiration, Potential Transformer

Experience: Outbound Sales & Leadership, Real Estate Innovation, Christian Leadership and Growth, Business Expansion, Personal Development Mastery

WITH A RICH BACKGROUND IN: Real Estate Investment, Healthcare and Medical Industry Strategies, Sales Excellence, Corporate Leadership Development

OFFERING ENGAGEMENTS: On-Site: $25,000 + Expenses, Virtual: $3,000 - $5,000

PROGRAM HIGHLIGHTS:

The Accelerator: Grow and Scale (90-Minute Keynote). Ideal for business owners and startup founders looking to catapult their ventures into new heights of success, this program arms you with Nathan's blueprint for rapid expansion and market dominance.

The CAESAR Method: Mastering Communication in Business (90-Minute Workshop). Designed for sales teams and entrepreneurs, this workshop unveils the secrets to impactful communication, ensuring every interaction is a step towards unparalleled success.

Small Multifamily Mastery: The 35 Red Flags You Need to Know (120-Minute Workshop). A must-attend for real estate investors and professionals, this workshop equips you with critical insights to navigate the multifamily investment landscape confidently.

Mind Renovation - Renovating Your Attitude (60-Minute Keynote). Perfect for professionals facing burnout or teams in need of a mindset overhaul, Nathan shares transformative strategies to foster resilience, positivity, and success.

How to You Can Achieve Double Digit Returns in Small Multifamily Real Estate. (Upto a 120-Minute Workshop).Discover how to secure double-digit returns in small multifamily real estate. Maximize your investment portfolio's potential with key strategies!

Nathan Bush is more than a speaker; he's an experience. His sessions are packed with actionable insights, grounded in real-world success, and delivered with the passion of someone who truly believes in the power of growth, leadership, and transformation. Join him, and let's unlock the potential within your team and your business together.

For speaking engagements and to learn more about how Nathan can inspire your team or audience, visit: https://linktr.ee/nathanbushmba.

Join The Disciples of Leadership Community

If you really would like your business to grow, please join me, Nathan Bush, and others in our Disciples of Leadership community on Facebook, a gathering place for those who aspire to lead with intention and integrity. Our community is dedicated to exploring the facets of leadership that transform not just businesses, but lives. It's about more than strategies and theories; it's about real-world application, accountability, and personal growth.

In Disciples of Leadership, you will transform your leadership so you can thrive as a disciple of leadership.

We train the principles that underpin successful leadership, share experiences, and support one another in our journeys. Whether you're a seasoned leader or just starting, this is a space to connect with peers, learn new concepts, and be inspired to take action.Follow this journey with me and become part of a vibrant group committed to excellence in leadership. Visit www.nathanbushmba.com/dol to join the Disciples of Leadership on Facebook. Let's grow together, learn together, and lead together. See you there!

Need a Strategic Growth Facilitator?

Let's have a real talk about your business's future. Imagine we're sitting down together over coffee, sharing stories about our journey in the world of business. You've got goals, big ones, and I can see the passion you have for what you do. It's clear you're not just playing the game; you're in it to redefine it. So, tell me, have you ever thought about what a strategy, one that's crafted just for you and your unique business, could do? Picture a growth plan that fits your company like a glove, tailored to highlight your strengths and set you on a path to not just reach but soar beyond your targets. That's what I'm here to chat with you about today.

Have you ever considered what a tailor-made growth strategy could do for your business? Are you seeking a method that not only understands your unique market position but also amplifies your strengths to drive success?

Introducing the CAESAR method – our proprietary framework for Strategic Growth Facilitation. This method is a synthesis of comprehensive market analysis, bespoke strategic planning, and continual adaptation, designed to position you at the forefront of your industry. By educating you on the CAESAR method, we empower you to understand the nuances of strategic growth, setting a clear intention to not just meet but exceed your ambitious business goals.

If these questions resonate with you, I invite you to set an appointment with me. Together, we'll explore how the CAESAR method can be the catalyst for your business's success. Begin this transformative journey at https://linktr.ee/nathanbushmba.

Using my alignment framework, we'll ensure that our collaboration is a perfect fit for your needs. We'll review your business's core objectives, align our services with your goals, and tailor a growth plan that resonates with your vision for success. This is not a one-size-fits-all approach; it's a roadmap designed to unlock your company's full potential. We can work with your leadership team, sales team, or marketing team, or all three or any combination.

If you know a business leader or organization that stands to benefit from the CAESAR method, please share this opportunity with them. Your referral is the highest compliment you can give us, and it's the cornerstone of our community's growth and success. We mean it when we say your success and that of your peers is our mission. Let's build a network of growth and achievement together.

Made in the USA
Monee, IL
15 March 2024

54550659R00089